God's Spirit in You

God's Spirit in You

Landrum P. Leavell

Broadman Press/Nashville, Tennessee

Library of Congress Catalog Card Number: 73–89526
Dewey Decimal Classification: 231.3
Printed in the United States of America

Dedication

To my parents
Mrs. Leonard O. Leavell
the late Dr. L. O. Leavell
who introduced me to
Jesus Christ, the Son of God
and lived their lives in the
Spirit before me

Preface

The chapters of this volume originally were sermons preached in the First Baptist Church, Wichita Falls, Texas. The series was prompted by what I felt to be a pressing need for a restudy of the teachings of the Bible, especially the New Testament, concerning the ministry of the Holy Spirit.

People are being told today that it is necessary to have a second experience of grace, a so-called "baptism" of the Holy Spirit accompanied by an ecstatic utterance in order to complete their salvation. The impression is often left that it is somehow better and superior to have this experience than it is to accept Jesus Christ as Savior and be born into the kingdom of God. This I construe to be a subtle form of blasphemy, for it relegates the living Christ to an inferior category. Since Jesus said the Holy Spirit would not speak of himself but would glorify Christ, I believe any teaching that exalts the Holy Spirit above Jesus Christ is a tragic departure from the New Testament.

It would be impossible to give credit to all who have contributed to my life and understanding. Insights, thoughts, and suggestions have come from innumerable sources, and I am deeply indebted to each of these though I cannot call each name.

One of life's greatest blessings is that of being the pastor of a church which constantly challenges and inspires me in the preaching of the Word. The members of First Baptist Church are among God's choicest saints, and no words are adequate to thank them for their love and understanding.

A personal word of appreciation is due my highly efficient secretary, Mrs. Tom Wilson, who has labored over this and other manuscripts, and never seems too busy to type something "one more time!"

This word is last, but really is first! God has blessed me with the ideal pastor's wife and four wonderful, very human preacher's kids. They love me even when I am irritable and in a hurry and they bring sunshine to my life every day.

I have used various translations, including my own translation, in addition to King James in the Scripture quotations in this book.

Landrum P. Leavell

Contents

Contents

1. The Spirit's Personality
JOHN 14:26

Nearly every adult can remember one toy most children formerly possessed. That toy was a kaleidoscope. We remember this instrument shaped like a telescope, containing fragments of colored glass which would move into beautiful symmetry with ever changing patterns. Holding it up to one's eye and directing it toward the light, the end could be turned so that these beautiful pieces of glass would fall into fantastically perfect designs.

There is no doctrine in the Bible more kaleidoscopic than the doctrine of the Holy Spirit. It contains beauty, symmetry, and reason. The Bible is a book of the Spirit. All the way through, from the very first page to the last, the Bible tells us of the Holy Spirit.

On the first page in the book of Genesis there is painted a somber picture of chaos over which the Spirit of God, like a mother bird hovering over a nest, brooded. On the last page of the Word of God, in the book of the Revelation, there is a ringing challenge to evangelism through the church: "And the Spirit and the bride say, Come." The Spirit, of course, is God himself and the bride is the body of the redeemed, the church of the Lord Jesus Christ. But all the way in between those two pages can be found the story of divine creativity. From God's standpoint it is revelation, from man's standpoint it is discovery.

We do well to understand that the Bible is not a book of minute historical events covering the total history of the Jewish people. The Bible rather describes outstanding events which were interpreted in the light of God's will as God's way of dealing with humanity to bring about his eternal purpose. God knew his will

11

from the beginning. He knew how he would deal with his people and he knew their rebellion, but God was constantly revealing himself and man was constantly seeking to discover God's purpose for his life. The Bible is uniquely a book of the Holy Spirit, yet we are in error if we try to know the works of the Holy Spirit before we know him.

I know many things about the life of George Washington; I know additional facts about the life of Abraham Lincoln, but I never knew either of these men personally. Let's not commit that error in regard to the Holy Spirit. Let's not seek simply to assimilate the truths concerning him, the facts about his ministry and his personality, but let's seek that warm, vital, indispensible relationship with him which we call regeneration, or the new birth.

Some people hold the erroneous concept that the Holy Spirit is merely an influence or a desire. The Bible makes no such statement. It's not possible for us to have a complete, well-rounded experience until we understand the personality of God's Holy Spirit.

I want to underscore some things about the Spirit. First I want us to remember the—

Attributes

—of the Holy Spirit. The Holy Spirit has all the attributes of human personality. The distinctive marks of personality are knowledge, feeling, and will. Don't confuse these with the physical body. A physical body is not necessary for these characteristics, but these characteristics are necessary for the animation of the physical body. The physical body, after life leaves it, is a lifeless corpse, but that does not mean the cessation of the marks of personality; knowledge, feeling, and will. Just because the human body ceases to function does not mean the personality ceases to exist. So I'm saying that the personality of the Holy Spirit is alive, virile, and active today in our world though not accompanied by a physical body. We do not see the Holy Spirit in physical terms as we see each other, but his personality does not require a physical body. His is spiritual, not physical, except as he is embodied in us.

In 2 Corinthians 5:8 we find the key to the answer to this dilemma. There we read "to be absent from the body [that is, for the Christian] . . . to be present with the Lord." The personality continues. These characteristics of man are created in the divine image; knowledge, feeling, will. We are made in God's own image and the personality, which is like God, is eternal, never dying. The body may die, but the personality continues to exist. We do not cease to be persons though the physical body may have ceased to function. The physical body is not essential to personality. With that in mind let's see what the Bible says about the attributes of the Holy Spirit.

First Corinthians 2:11 tells us that the Holy Spirit *knows*. This is knowledge. He knows as a person. "For what man knoweth the things of man save the spirit of man which is in him? Even so the things of God knoweth no man, but the Spirit of God." God the Holy Spirit knows. He has knowledge. He has knowledge of the things of God and he reveals those things to the minds of human beings.

Who was the best Sunday School teacher you've ever had? Immediately a name or names come to mind. They could well be, and may be, the names of persons who had little formal education. Yet they were well schooled in the things of the Spirit. How does this come about? It comes about because the Holy Spirit knows the things of God and reveals the things of God to those who seek them. The Holy Spirit imparts knowledge, not on the basis of our accomplishments, not on the basis of our educational credentials, but on the basis of our spiritual credentials. He knows and reveals what he knows.

Again, 1 Corinthians 12:11 tells us that the Holy Spirit *wills* as a person. Here it is: "But the one and same Spirit accomplishes all these achievements, and apportions power to each of us as he chooses." You have the power of choice. You have the power of will. You attend church because you choose to. You will to be there. By that same token, the Holy Spirit has will. He apportions spiritual gifts. He chooses persons to receive spiritual gifts. He does not do this in an arbitrary manner. God has not decreed: "Out of every 25 human beings I'm going to give one the power of prophecy. I'm going to give one out of every 22 human beings the gift of divine healing. Out of every 135 human beings I'm going to give one the gift of evangelism, and out of every 795 humans I'm going to give one the gift of teaching." Not at all. It's not done in an arbitrary manner. It rather is done deliberately and discriminately, according to the surrender and the capacity of the believer. In other words, the Holy Spirit will give you only what you are capable of handling! If you don't meet the terms that God has established in dedication and commitment, God will not trust you with his spiritual gifts.

Ephesians 4:11 tells us that he gives some prophets, some apostles, some pastors, some evangelists, some teachers. But he gives these gifts on the basis of our surrender and our willingness to do whatever he has in mind for us.

I have told our young people to never, never, never pray to "get" the Holy Spirit. Don't ever pray that prayer as a Christian. The only prayer that you and I ought to pray is that he will always, always, always, always get us! When he gets us, he can give us what he will! Don't you dare beg God, like a spoiled child, for one of God's gifts. If God wants you to have that gift, he'll give it to you without your begging for it! If you meet his conditions, he'll provide for you. You don't have to beg him for something good. He's not that kind of God. He's willing to give you everything good he's got if you give him everything you've got.

The Holy Spirit knows like a person, he wills like a person, and in Romans 8:27 we read that the Holy Spirit *feels* like a person. The verse states: "And he that searcheth the hearts knoweth what is the mind of the Spirit." Now this word "mind" is the important one, m-i-n-d, for in the Greek it has particular significance. The word translated "mind" in the original language carries the idea of knowledge, feeling, and will. The Holy Spirit *feels* our needs and the Holy Spirit *fills* our needs. He knows our needs before we do. He knows every facet of truth that's knowable. Nothing is hidden from him.

The space program of the Americans and the Russians in the 60's and 70's came as no surprise to the Holy Spirit. We didn't catch God off guard with our space probes. God had that knowledge from the beginning and has just been waiting for man to gain enough knowledge to uncover the secrets that made this possible.

God could be likened in this sense to a professor with a Ph.D. in math who sits to watch his child working on a math problem. His child, in the first grade, is laboriously, with gravest difficulty, trying to work out this math problem. And finally the child's face brightens and he looks up and says: "I've got it. Two plus two equals four." The father, with his learning, with his advanced degree in mathematics, smiles indulgently, delighted that his child has learned one of the basic rudiments of mathematics.

God the Father is like that. God the Holy Spirit is like that. He knows everything that's knowable. There is nothing that man will ever discover that's going to take God by surprise. There is no facet of truth man will ever uncover that's going to negate God. God knows all the facts and through the Holy Spirit he seeks to reveal his facts to the hearts of human beings.

Think about this: Jesus Christ is interceding for us in heaven. He knows us, knows everything there is about us, and here on earth the Holy Spirit is interceding for us in our hearts. How can a child of God be unhappy or morose?

Now we'll notice some—

Attitudes

—in the personality of the Spirit.

In Romans 15:30 we find the blessed truth that the Holy Spirit *loves*. Have you thought about that? "Now I beseech you, brethren, for the Lord Jesus Christ's sake, and for the love of the Spirit, that ye strive together with me in your prayers to God for me." For the love of the Spirit. We talk a great deal about the love of the Father and the love of Jesus the Son, but it was the love of the Holy Spirit that caused him to seek out you and me in sin, to convict our hearts of iniquity, and by divine power to regenerate us and perform God's redemptive work in our hearts! It's the love of the Spirit that continues to seek out humanity.

Somewhere back across the years I encountered a poem by Francis Thompson. The title of it was "The Hound of Heaven," and in this poem the Holy Spirit is described as a hound on the trail, always seeking, always following, never giving up, "down through the labyrinthine ways of time," Thompson said. And so it is in the work of God, because of the love of the Holy Spirit seeking us out until ultimately he finds us, and our hearts are opened and he convicts us and makes us new in the likeness and image of Jesus Christ.

In Ephesians 4:30 we find that we can *grieve* the Spirit. "And grieve not the holy Spirit of God whereby ye are sealed unto the day of redemption." How do you or I grieve the Spirit? We grieve him by the sins of the flesh and the sins of the spirit, by sins of omission and sins of commission. Any compromise of God's standard of righteousness established in Jesus Christ grieves the Spirit.

Paul said in Romans 3:23, "For all have sinned, and come short of the glory of God." The glory of God is Jesus. He's God's standard of righteousness. Anything we are, anything we do that is less than that standard of absolute perfection is sin. We come short of the glory of God and in coming short we grieve the Holy Spirit.

In 1 Thessalonians 5:19 we learn that it's possible to *quench* the Holy Spirit. "Quench not the Spirit." Now you can quench him without expelling him.

I can recall numerous occasions when I had to quench a member of my family! I had to tell one on occasion: "That's all I want to hear about that. Let's don't talk about it anymore. Hush. No more." Now I quench them in that way, but that's not to be made synonymous with expulsion. I don't expel them. I don't kick them out of the house. I just quench them. "Let's don't talk about that any more. I don't want to hear any more about it."

That same thing happens in our relationship to the Holy Spirit. We can quench him without expelling him. You see, if we are true believers he never leaves us. The Holy Spirit is never expelled from the life of a true believer, but we quench him when we suppress or stifle him. Now honestly, have you quenched the Spirit in this way? Have you ever said: "Lord, I don't want to know anything more about it. Lord, don't keep on worrying me about tithing. Lord, I don't intend to be a preacher. Lord, I don't want to be a missionary. Let me alone! Don't keep worrying me with these things."

Is there some facet of your life that needs to be brought under the scrutiny of the Holy Spirit that you have held back from him? You've quenched him! You've said no. You've refused to let his penetrating power come into that part of your life.

There are habits that you have about which you say, "Lord, quit worrying me about this." Maybe it's those cancerous cigarettes and you know they are harmful. You don't have to be told that. You don't need a doctor's report or a report of the Surgeon General. You know they don't help your feelings and they don't help your physical body. You know that. Maybe it's pills you are on. Maybe it's whiskey you're drinking, but you are saying to the Lord: "Lord, quit worrying me about this. Let me alone! I don't want to hear any more about it!" Now, if you are a true believer, the Holy Spirit is in your heart but you have quenched him. You haven't expelled him. You can't get rid of him if you are a true believer, but you can surely quench him and keep his voice from being heard.

The Holy Spirit is referred to in the Bible as "fire." There are many instances where the Holy Spirit is likened to fire. You know, you can quench a fire in three ways. One way is to leave it alone, and that's neglect. That's just indifference. If the fire of the Holy

Spirit is in your heart and you're indifferent and neglectful, you quench him.

Maybe you say: "No, I'm not a Sunday nighter, and I don't intend to be a Sunday nighter! I have other things to do on Sunday night. No, I don't go to prayer meeting. I don't intend to go to prayer meeting!" You quench him. Why don't you ask him what he wants you to do?

Let me suggest something else. If he gives you permission not to come on Sunday night, then don't you come. If he tells you it's all right not to come on Wednesday night, go ahead and do what you do on Wednesday. It'll be all right, but I say if you haven't asked him, if you haven't put your life in openness under his direction, then you are quenching him. Neglect.

I read a statement that said the opposite of love is not hate. The opposite of love is indifference. That gets down close to where we live, doesn't it? The opposite of love is indifference. Who cares?

You can quench a fire by leaving it alone. You can also quench a fire by pouring water on it. That's willful sin. That is when there is something in your life you know is wrong, that ought not to be a part of your life, and you continue to do it regardless. You have said to God, "I'm going to do this no matter what!" You quench the Spirit when you do.

A third way to put out a fire is by putting noncombustible material on it. You can smother it that way. You can put asbestos all over a fire and it won't be a fire very long. That is worldliness and selfishness in the life of a Christian. That's when you say: "I'm the master of my fate. I am the captain of my soul. I'll do it my way!" When you do, you quench the Holy Spirit.

Acts 5:3 tells us that we can *lie* to the Holy Spirit. "But Peter said, Ananias, why hath Satan filled thy heart to lie to the Holy Spirit?" What was his lie? His lie was he had told everybody that he was doing something he wasn't doing. He told everybody he was giving his all, but he wasn't. Are you playacting? That's what a hypocrite is, when you're acting like you are giving your all and you really are not.

Now remember some of the—

Actions

—of the Holy Spirit. Let's remember first of all Romans 8:26 where we find that the Holy Spirit *prays.* "And in like manner also the Spirit helpeth our infirmity, for we know not how to pray as we ought, but the Spirit himself. . . ." Listen, that's a personal pronoun, not neuter. King James has an error right there as far as the original is concerned. In the Greek language that's always a masculine pronoun, personal, himself. "The Spirit *himself* maketh intercession for us with groanings."

Are you one of those who over a period of years has said: "I just don't feel like God is hearing my prayers. I try to pray and it just doesn't do any good." Don't get upset about that. You don't have anything to worry about. That's when the Holy Spirit takes over. When you feel as though you can't get through to God, turn it over to him. He'll make the intercession for you with groanings. He knows you, he knows everything about you, he knows your need, and he will fill your need. Let him do the praying for you. You just stand there, sit there, or lie there and cry out unto God. He knows what's in your heart and don't you ever think he doesn't hear you, because when your prayer is ended the Holy Spirit's prayer begins, and I can guarantee you that God will hear the prayer of the Spirit. The Holy Spirit prays.

John 14:26, our text, tells us that he *teaches.* "But the Comforter, even the Holy Spirit, whom the Father will send in My Name, He shall teach you all things." Listen, you are privileged today to sit under the tutelage of the world's greatest, most knowledgeable teacher. "If any lack wisdom, let him ask of God, who giveth liberally and upbraideth not." In other words, ask God for wisdom and he's not going to fuss at you and say, "What do you want wisdom for?" He's going to give it to you liberally. Ask him for wisdom and see what he'll do for you. It's under his direction that the Bible comes alive.

In John 14:16–17 we read and learn that the Spirit *comforts.* "And I'll pray the Father and He'll give you another Comforter." In other words, the Holy Spirit came to take the place of Jesus and to do what Jesus had done when he was here on earth.

The disciples came to Jesus and said, "Lord, teach us to pray," and he did. You ask the Holy Spirit to teach you to pray and he will! Peter asked the Lord to bid him to do the impossible, to walk on the water, and Jesus did. Ask Jesus to give you the power to do the impossible for his honor and the upbuilding of his Kingdom, and he will.

Is your problem fear? He provides courage and strength. Is your problem loneliness? He can fill any void. Is your problem some debilitating habit? Listen, friend, he'll give you the victory. Is your problem sin? He applies the blood of Jesus Christ which cleanseth us from all sin. All that's left for you and me to do is to come to him, to open our lives to his direction and to allow him to lead us daily and hourly.

2. The Spirit's Power
JOHN 16:6–11

Many have sounded a warning against our neglect of the Holy Spirit. Dr. E. Y. Mullins, a great theologian among Southern Baptists in a bygone generation, said, "It's a strange and significant fact that Christians for nearly two thousand years have so generally neglected the New Testament teaching concerning the Holy Spirit." Dr. A. W. Tozer said, "In most Christian churches the Holy Spirit is entirely overlooked. Whether he is present or absent makes no real difference to anyone. Brief reference is made to him in the invocation and the benediction, and further than that he might as well not exist." I wonder how true that statement is.

Dr. Carl F. H. Henry said, "The most displaced person of the twentieth century is the Holy Spirit." Dr. John Owens said, "The sin of the Old Testament was rejecting God the Father; the sin of the New Testament was rejecting God, the Son; the sin of the church age is rejecting God, the Holy Spirit."

Generally speaking there are two separate and distinct aspects of the Christian faith. One of these is historical. I refer to that body of knowledge that can be assimilated by reading, by studying, by hearing sermons or lectures, or by sharing with friends. You may learn historical facts in this way.

I'm certain there is hardly a person who does not know the historical facts concerning the life of Jesus Christ; that he lived, that he was crucified, that he died, and that he rose from the grave. This body of material is objective. It comes to us from without. It is one aspect of the Christian faith.

But there is a second, and this is the one largely overlooked by

21

church members in general. This one we call experiential or, as some modern philosophers have chosen to name it, existential. This refers to something that has taken place personally. In referring to this body of knowledge we ask not, "do you know," but, "have you experienced?" This body of material or this area of knowledge is true because it happened to us. There is no person on the face of the earth who can refute your personal experience. No one can say to you, "This did not happen to you." You're the world's only authority on this body of knowledge. You're the one to whom it happened. This body of knowledge is subjective, for it comes from within.

Both aspects of the Christian faith are valid. The Christian faith is not complete without both. It is never enough for a Christian to say, "I know this because I read it." It's always vital for a Christian to say, "I know this because it has happened to me."

You can go out in your efforts to lead lost people to Christ and share with them the truths you have found in the pages of God's Word, and you'll learn, to your dismay, that the people are unimpressed. On the other hand, when you go to say to a person, "I want to share with you the greatest thing that ever took place in my life," the chances are that person will sit up and take notice and listen to what you have to say.

Every American knows about Richard Milhouse Nixon. There are not many of us, though, who can say, "I know him." I personally know about him, but I do not know him. Not many of us can say: "I have been a friend of his across many years. He and I have eaten together, we've slept under the same roof, and we've fellowshipped through the hours of the day. I've known him for a long, long time." But there is a real difference in knowing about Richard Nixon and knowing Richard Nixon personally. There is a great deal of difference between knowing about the Holy Spirit and knowing him.

It was interesting in speaking to a youth worship, to ask them questions and expect a response from the audience. I am grateful that there was a response! I asked those young people, "What do you know about the Holy Spirit?" If I were to ask you that question and tell you to write the answer on a piece of paper, would your paper be blank? What do you know about him?

Then I asked the question, "What has the Holy Spirit ever done for you?" I don't believe it's possible to be saved and not have some inkling of what the Holy Spirit can and will do in the life of a believer. You may not know how this has come about, but you must be aware of the fact that it has happened. When the Holy Spirit touches your heart and you become a new creature in Christ, you may not be able to explain it theologically, but you positively can tell that it has occurred experientially.

Jack Taylor has written two books now on the work and ministry of the Holy Spirit. He's a pastor in San Antonio but probably his main claim to fame is that he is kin to Bill and Juanita Baird. Jack's second book is titled, *Much More*. In it he makes some observations that I'd like to pass on to you. "The Christian life is an event followed by a process." Did you know that? Are you living like you know it? It is an event followed by a process! The event is when you renounce sin and receive Jesus Christ. The process involves the remainder of your life on this earth.

Then he wrote, "It is an experience followed by a relationship." Did you know that? The relationship is living in Christ day by day as long as he lets you live on the face of this earth. It's all predicated on the experience, but it's a relationship that is never broken.

He also wrote, "It is a step followed by a walk." Now a lot of you have made the step. You've received Jesus Christ as your Savior, but are you walking the walk? You see, the Christian faith is both. It is a step *of* faith and it is a walk *in* faith day by day. That's where the Holy Spirit comes in.

You don't know much about the Christian faith if all you know is the initial experience by which you say: "I repent of my sins and, right now, I take Jesus as my Savior." You can make that step and remain a spiritual pygmy all your life. You must come to understand that the Christian faith is a step and a walk.

Then Jack Taylor made this statement, "It is an act followed by an appropriation." It is an act of God by which we become new creatures in Christ, and then it is a daily appropriation of the power of God for Christian living. Did you know that? I knew it, but I never had put it in these words. I wish I had said that. Many a believer has stopped with the event, the experience, the step, the act, and has never gone on to maturity. He has lived a life of spiritual poverty and spiritual defeat, always under suspicion that there was much more. Thank you, Jack Taylor, for reminding us of that. Thank you for reminding us not to stop with the event, the initial experience, but reminding us to go on to maturity, to go on to much more.

Are you one of those Christians who has a dark brown taste in your mouth, wondering if maybe there isn't something you've missed? Friend, I want to tell you that's a spiritual hunger that God puts in your heart! If you really do know him, if you've made the step, if this act has transpired within you, then there is a hungering and a thirsting for more! That thirsting can only be satisfied when Jesus Christ takes hold of your life and by the power of the Holy Spirit leads you daily to be what Christ would be if he were living in your flesh, occupying your job, residing under your roof, and if he had the opportunities spiritually that you have. That's the appropriation. That's the walk. That's the process in which you become by the power of the Holy Spirit, what Jesus would be if Jesus were encased in your body.

Do you know the Holy Spirit? If you're saved you must, for there is no other way of salvation. Now, I'm not asking you if you know about Jesus. I'm asking do you know him? Is it personal with you? Is it a moment-by-moment existence in faith? Maybe someone asks, "Well, how can I know him?" I propose to answer that on the basis of truths gleaned from the Word of God and my own experience. The agent who makes it possible for us to know the living Christ is the Holy Spirit and he's here today. We see his work and his power first in—

Conviction.

He is to convict the world of sin, of righteousness, and of judgment. I don't suppose there are many people but who already know that. It's the words of our text. Jesus said that when the Holy Spirit has come, he'll convict the world of sin, of righteousness, and of judgment.

Then he went on to explain it. Of sin, because they robbed banks! Is that what he said? No. Of sin, because they commit adultery! No. Of sin, because they believe not on me! That's the sin of which the Holy Spirit convicts.

You talk to the average lost man, and what does he say? "I'm living as good a life as any member of your church," and he probably is. The sin, however, is that he has rejected Jesus Christ, and that's the sin that sends a man to hell. You don't go to hell because you committed adultery. Jesus can forgive that sin. You don't go to hell for robbing banks. Jesus forgives that sin if you ask him. You don't go to hell because you've done all of the mean things that the world knows. God can forgive those sins. But the one sin he can't forgive is your sin of rejecting Jesus. He can't forgive it if you won't let him, for he won't come into your life and forgive a sin that you don't want forgiven.

So the lost world needs to know that they are condemned to go to hell, not because they are bad, but because they have rejected Jesus. The lost world needs to know that we are not going to go to heaven because we're good. We're not! We are going to go to Heaven because we have trusted Jesus. The Holy Spirit is the one who makes us know this. He convicts the world of sin, "because they believe not on me."

The worst thing you can do is not to commit murder, the worst thing you do is to reject Jesus. Now I'm not condoning murder.

I'm not urging you to go out and kill somebody. I'm saying the worst thing you can do is to reject what God has offered you in Jesus Christ. The Holy Spirit is the convicting agent making us know this.

How many times have you heard someone say: "The preacher really was preaching to me today," or, "The preacher sure stepped on my toes." I don't know whose toes are being stepped on. All that I know is that God gives me a message he wants preached, and when I preach it the convicting is up to him. I'm not responsible for the convicting. That's his job and if I try, in human strength, to convict you of where you are wrong, it isn't going to work. All I have to do is be faithful in preaching the Word and he does the convicting. He hasn't called me to convict. He's called me to preach, and all I need to do is to be faithful in doing what God called me to do and he takes care of the rest of it. If you've been conscience smitten at any point in your life during the preaching of the Word of God, it was the Spirit of God that quickened your mind and not the preacher that you happened to have heard preach.

The only way any human being can ever be saved is to know that he's lost. Jesus said, "They that be whole need not a physician, but they that are sick." In other words He was saying a well man doesn't need a doctor. Only sick people need doctors. The person who doesn't know he is lost doesn't feel any need for a Savior. It's only when a man becomes burdened by his sin and realizes that the worst thing he's ever done is to turn his back upon Jesus Christ and the call of the church and the Kingdom in this world, then he can turn to Christ and find peace and joy in his heart. Only the Holy Spirit can convict a man of this need.

Every soul-winner who goes out to share his faith feels a deep sense of inadequacy because he knows he's merely a witness. He's there to sow the seed, but the Spirit has to take the seed and plant it in the heart of the lost person and bring forth the harvest for the honor of Jesus.

Any presentation of the way of salvation that does not include conviction and repentance for sin is spurious. That's the reason I do not give my personal assent to the promiscuous use of these so-called "four spiritual laws." You can lead a person to say yes on the basis of those four spiritual laws, but there is no mention there of repentance. A person who says yes to something before he's ever known that he's a guilty sinner and that he must repent of sin can't be saved. You don't get saved by saying yes to the fact that there's a historical person named Jesus. You get saved when you understand that you've sinned against him and that the biggest sin you've committed is turning your back on him. Then when you, in brokenhearted remorse, turn from that sin you can be saved. You can't be saved until you know you're lost. The Holy Spirit is the one who convicts of sin.

Then there's a second thing. We see the power of the Holy Spirit in—

Conversion.

Jesus said to Nicodemus: "Except a man be born again he cannot enter into the kingdom of God." Now in theological or ministerial language this is called regeneration, or the new birth. This is called being born again. This is something God does, and it's not something that man does.

Physical life begins at the moment of physical birth. You begin to live when you're born. That's just as true spiritually as it is physically. You don't begin to live spiritually until you've been born spiritually, and unless you've been born spiritually or born again, unless you've had the new birth, you cannot see the kingdom of God! It all begins when you repent of your sins and trust Jesus Christ as your Savior.

Now when the new birth takes place, that is an act of God by which we become new creatures, our natures are changed and our destinies are reversed. Instead of living for what we can get, we begin living for what we can give.

Sam Jones was a great Methodist evangelist in a bygone era. He used this analogy. Take a dog and put him in the house, bathe him, perfume him, put a ribbon around his neck, and treat him like a human being. Yet when you turn your back on him he'll still act like a dog. Let him out the door and he wallows in the dirt. He'll still be a dog no matter how you might fix him up on the outside. The only way he'll ever be anything other than a dog is for his nature to be changed.

Man will always be a lost sinner until his nature is changed. Then he still is a sinner, but he is a saved sinner. By nature, he's no longer headed to hell, he's headed to heaven. God by his own power fixes a man up in an act that we call the new birth. This is the conversion experience. It does not have to be synonymous with the conversion of Paul. You don't have to have a Damascus Road experience, but the experience you have has to be a real one. You have to mean it. You have to commit your life to Christ and you have to be willing to live for him daily, giving an indication to the world that you have been born again. "By their fruits ye shall know them."

Can a person belong to the church without having been born again? Yes. Yes, because the church is not the door to salvation. The church is the gateway to service, and there are a lot of people who have volunteered for service who have never joined the army. They've never been inducted. You must be inducted before you can be in Christ's army, and the induction is called the new birth. You can put on the uniform and not be a member of his army. You can put on the cloak of righteousness which we call church membership and know nothing about a new life, a new nature given by the power of God.

The way to conversion is to run up the white flag of total surrender. When you do, needing the Physician, knowing that you're sick, the Physician comes and you are healed, you're made new, you're given this new nature.

Then, there is a third step. In addition to conviction and conversion, we see the power of the Holy Spirit in—

Consecration.

A close study of the New Testament doctrine of sanctification leads us to the assurance that this is an experience performed by the power of God. There are a lot of erroneous ideas about sanctification abroad in our world. There are some people who think they get sanctified when they quit wearing lipstick and rouge, when they quit wearing earrings and bracelets, and rings on their fingers. There are some men who think they are sanctified when they quit smoking cigarettes or cigars. Well, I think in most cases sanctification might involve that sort of thing, but the point is, sanctification is not something you do, sanctification is something God does for you.

In 1 Peter 1:2: "Elect according to the foreknowledge of God the Father, through sanctification of the Spirit, unto obedience." It's something the Spirit does for you when you obey him.

In 1 Corinthians 6:11: "And such were some of you: but ye are washed, but ye are sanctified, but ye are justified in the name of the Lord Jesus, and by the Spirit of our God." It's something God's Spirit does for us.

In 2 Thessalonians 2:13: "But we are bound to give thanks alway to God for you, brethren beloved of the Lord, because God hath from the beginning chosen you to salvation through sanctification of the Spirit and belief of the truth." Who does the sanctifying? Do you do it with your little pious scissors when you clip off all the things that you think God doesn't like? No, you just turn it over to him and let him do the clipping. When you turn it over to him in entirety, do anything he permits you to do. Do anything he authorizes. Keep on doing any of the things in your life that he says are permissible. He sanctifies.

It isn't something you do, because that would produce spiritual pride. Some of the proudest people I know are those Christians who think that they have arrived, for they somehow do not understand that one of the besetting sins of God's people is the sin of pride.

What's the basic difference in church members? Why are some consecrated and some not? The difference is found in our submission to the leadership and direction of the Holy Spirit. We read in John 16:13–14: "When he, the Spirit of truth, is come, he will guide you into all truth. . . . He shall glorify me: for he shall receive of mine, and shall shew it unto you."

Let's ask some questions. Does a Spirit-filled Christian rob God of his tithe? Will a Spirit-directed Christian be indifferent to training in church membership and growth in grace? Do you think a committed soldier in the army of Jesus Christ would say: "Now, I'll serve, but I'll serve when I want to. I don't want to train and I don't want to try to learn anything new. I want to just do what I'm doing."

Will a Spirit-filled Christian give the impression that prayer meeting is anathema? Would a Spirit-filled Christian be indifferent to lost people all about him? Will a Spirit-filled Christian hold grudges, bear hatreds, animosity, or ill will toward other people? These are questions that point up the deficiencies in our lives, and they indicate rather clearly whether or not we are Spirit-filled and Spirit-empowered.

So the big question is: "Does the Holy Spirit have me? Has the Christ of history ever become the Christ of personal experience?" Can you be saved and know it? Absolutely yes. There is only one way, however, and that's for you to surrender your will and make Jesus Lord. You'll never be consecrated and have the joy of salvation until you've been convicted and converted. That's God's way and we can make it our way through submission to it.

There's a song that we used to sing when I was younger. The words went like this:

Are there any rivers that seem to be uncrossable?
   Are there any mountains you cannot tunnel through?
God specializes in things that seem impossible,
   He knows a million ways to make a way for you.

Let go and let God have His wonderful way,
   Let go and let God have His way,
Your burdens will vanish, your night turn to day,
   Let go and let God have His way.

3. The Spirit's Presence
HEBREWS 13:5

In two preceding chapters we have considered vital aspects of the work and ministry of the Holy Spirit. We have underscored the fact of his personality, for he has mind, feeling, and will. These are the distinctive marks of personality as we know it, and the Holy Spirit is a person.

We've also dealt with the power of the Holy Spirit, for we need to know what he does in the life of a believer. There are those things God has assigned to us for which we are responsible, and there are those things for which God is responsible based upon our response.

God's promise of salvation is conditional. It's conditioned upon man's response to God's offer. There are cases in the Bible in which God has made unconditional promises. One of these is, "I will send rain upon the just and upon the unjust." It doesn't make any difference what man's response is, God has promised to do that. God has not required that we be faithful in order to receive rain.

But in other cases, throughout the Word of God, he has said, "If you'll do this, I'll do this." Second Chronicles 7:14 is one conditional promise that comes to mind. "If my people, which are called by my name, shall humble themselves, and pray, and seek my face . . . then will I hear from heaven." The promise of the power of the Holy Spirit in the life of a believer is conditional. God has never said, "I'll give you my salvation and my power, no matter what." We are required to meet God's conditions, and these are the matters we have considered in two preceding studies on the doctrine of the Holy Spirit.

32

Have you ever lost a needed article? One of the most frustrating experiences that has been mine in raising a family has been that of being unable to keep up with my tools. Any time I need a pair of pliers I go to the place where I keep my tools, but the chances are excellent that the pliers are not there, but out in the grass in the backyard. If I happen to need a screwdriver, the one I need is always missing. In order for a tool to be useful and functional, you have to know where it is, be able to get it, to locate it, and then you can use it.

In that same sense I believe that it's important for us to know where the Holy Spirit is if he's to use us, if we're to derive the strength and the power he makes available to us. So I invite you to think about the Holy Spirit's presence. We're as dependent upon him in our spiritual lives and usefulness as we're dependent upon breath in our physical lives. Unless we breathe, take in and exhale oxygen and the other elements in the air, we'll not live long. Unless we derive the strength and power the Holy Spirit makes available to us in the spiritual life, we'll fail to be active and useful.

I want to remind you first of Christ's—

Covenant.

Just as surely as God made a covenant with Abraham in the Old Testament, Christ made a covenant with his followers in the New Testament. God said to Abraham, "I will bless thee and make thee a blessing." That was a covenant God never broke.

In the New Testament Jesus Christ has made a covenant with you and me, as well as with every follower of his from the beginning until he comes again. That covenant is found in many places in the Word of God, and though the words may be slightly different, the meaning is exactly the same.

In the Great Commission Jesus said, "And lo, I am with you alway, even unto the end of the world." There in Matthew 28:19–20 Jesus said to his church, to you and me, "As ye go disciple all nations, baptizing them in the name of the Father, the Son and

the Holy Spirit, teaching them to observe all things whatsoever I
have commanded you, and lo, I am with you alway." That covenant has never been retracted.

As long as we're involved in the fulfillment of the Great Commission, as long as a church is giving itself to the consummation
of this divine strategy, Jesus Christ never leaves us nor forsakes
us.

Again in John 14:18, Jesus said, "I will not leave you comfort-
less, I will come unto you."

In Hebrews 13:5, Jesus said, "I will never leave thee, nor forsake
thee." This is a divine covenant repeated at least three different
times in the New Testament. It's a covenant with believers. Jesus
has never broken his promise. Now this is an elementary truth, but
it needs to be underscored. Jesus Christ is of unimpeachable integrity. He is sinlessly perfect. Jesus Christ has never broken his word.
He promised never to leave us, therefore, his covenant is valid
today.

It's for that reason that I have suggested that it's like "carrying
coals to Newcastle" for a Christian to pray to "get" the Holy Spirit.
That should never be our prayer. If you understand the Christian
faith, if you've been born into the family of God, the Holy Spirit
has taken up residence in your heart and he'll never, never leave
you. You don't have to pray to "get" the Holy Spirit, you have
to pray for the Holy Spirit to "get" you. The fact of the matter
is, he can't "get" you if the devil's got you. If the devil is riding
in the driver's seat in your life, the Holy Spirit cannot get you. You
are the one who has to say no to the devil in order to say yes to
the Holy Spirit. So don't pray to get the Holy Spirit, pray that he'll
get you. Pray that you'll have enough courage to say no to temptation and known sin. He'll never leave the true believer. Therefore,
our prayer ought to be that he who dwells within us shall possess
us. When sin ceases to control us, then the Holy Spirit can control
us.

In preaching to our youth I have suggested the possibility that a young person might come by my house in his Volkswagen and ask me to go for a ride. I would agree and get in the Volkswagen on the rider's side and we would start. I'd say, "Where are we going?" Maybe he would reply, "Where do you want to go?" I'd respond, "I'd like to go down to the corner of Ninth and Burnett, 1200 Ninth Street, to the First Baptist Church." Then maybe we'd ride for a few minutes and he'd suddenly say, "I don't think that's where I want to go. I want to go out Southwest Parkway." As long as he's driving and I'm riding, I might be resident in that automobile but I am not the driver, and I would simply have to go where the driver took me. The Holy Spirit may be in your life and not in the driver's seat. He cannot be unless you get out of the driver's seat and say, "Here, you drive, I'm going to ride." When you make that simple, elementary commitment, when you take your hands off the steering wheel of your life and allow him to control you, then you can pray for the fullness of the power of the Holy Spirit and that fullness will be yours. Don't pray to get the Holy Spirit, pray for the Holy Spirit to get you.

Never forget Christ's covenant. He said he'd never leave us. We may be going in the wrong direction from the direction that he wants us to take. We may be on a detour when he wants us on the Interstate, but he doesn't leave. He doesn't jump out at the first corner when we slow down. He remains a resident in the heart of a true believer. If you have been born again, the Spirit of the living God never leaves you for one instant. He may not be in control, but he's there, ready to take over if you, by your own self determination and discipline, refuse to let the devil control you and allow God to control you. His covenant is that he'll be there, and he's ready any moment to control you.

Now this is the covenant. Refresh your memory, if you will, with the Christian—

Calling.

In Romans 8:9 Paul said that if a man did not have the Spirit of God, that man does not belong to God. Therefore, the Holy Spirit is present in the heart of every true believer. If the Holy Spirit is not present in your life, whether or not he's in control, if he's not present in your life, you're not a Christian. But if he is present, it's because you've repented of your sins and put your faith and trust in the Lord Jesus Christ.

Again in Romans 8:14, Paul said, "As many as are led by the Spirit of God, they are the sons of God." The proof of the pudding is whether or not you allow him to drive. If he's not in control there is some question, isn't there? I don't mean that you'll be sinlessly perfect, but I mean that when the Spirit of God drives, you'll be heading in the right direction. You are not going to be wandering back and forth. You may stumble, you may fall, but if the Spirit of God is in control, you'll stand again, brush yourself off and keep moving! There won't be any doubt in your mind as to whose side you're on and whether or not God is with you.

In Romans 8:16 Paul said, "The Spirit [himself] beareth witness with our spirit, that we are the children of God." Can a man be saved and know it? Absolutely and positively yes!

After a recent sermon, a man called me on the telephone and said, "Preacher, I believe what you were preaching today is the height of presumption." I said, "What do you mean?" He said, "I think it is the height of presumption for a man to say that he's saved and that he knows he's saved." That may have been his true attitude, but his attitude was based on ignorance, because he simply does not know the promises of the Word of God. Can a Christian be saved and know it? Yes, beyond any peradventure of a doubt. The reason we know is that the Holy Spirit dwells in the life of a believer, infusing the personality of God into the life of an individual.

I can see some dramatic changes that have taken place in my life that could only be a tribute to the presence of the living God. I think of prejudices that I have held in life, growing up as I did in the deep South, and I can see a dramatic about-face that has taken place, not because I thought it through and decided this was right and humanitarian, but because I became convicted that under God, I had no right to feel differently toward a man whose skin is not the same color as mine.

Some friends from Mississippi, whom I have known for twenty or more years, stopped by briefly on their way home. As you might imagine the first question they asked was, "Is your church integrated?" I smiled and said yes. They began to look at each other and then at me and asked: "What do you think about this? How do you feel about it?" I replied: "I'll tell you where I reached the irreducible minimum. I fought through this thing, this matter of prejudice, until I finally concluded that if this church is Christ's church, I have no right to turn away anybody that Christ would not turn away."

How do you reach conclusions and decisions like this? By the power of the living God in the heart of a believer. This isn't something you suddenly decide. The absolution of prejudices that you've held through many years, your attitude toward people considered beneath you or in a different economic class than you—you don't just come automatically to those decisions. The Spirit of God, working in the heart of a believer, leads one to such a place. The Spirit dwells in the life of a believer. Where is he? He is in your heart if you really are saved.

We don't possess him, we don't pray to get him, for that would imply that humanity can manipulate deity. It rather ought to be the prayer of every sincere follower of Christ that he will possess or "get" us, and he will when we become submissive to his touch. He and he alone can direct us to the fulfillment of the Christian calling.

There are two verses of Scripture that seem to point up specifically the calling of the Christian. One of these is 1 Corinthians 3:16: "Know ye not that ye are the temple of God, and that the Spirit of God dwelleth in you?" Now that has a lot to do with your calling.

I don't believe every Christian is called to preach or serve in a full-time, church-related vocation. I don't believe that the closer you get to God, the more likely you are to become a missionary. Not necessarily, but I believe that there is a Christian calling to which every follower of Christ must give himself. If the Spirit of God controls you, you'll give yourself.

Again, in 1 Corinthians 16:9: "What, know ye not that your body is the temple of the Holy Spirit which is in you, which ye have of God, and ye are not your own!" Now, brother, that has to do with the Christian calling whether you are an ordained preacher or not.

Dr. Havner once said he was preaching in a church when it became unbearably hot in the pulpit. He began to mop his brow with his handkerchief, and was perspiring profusely. Now, for you who are uninformed, that means he was sweating pretty freely. After a few moments he turned and looked at some men seated over on the side of the building and asked, "Would one of you please lift a window?" He went on preaching, but nobody moved. In a few minutes he looked over there again and asked, "Would one of you fellows mind raising a window?" Nobody moved. He kept on preaching, but finally stopped in exasperation and said, "You don't have to be ordained to open a window!"

You don't have to be ordained to be called of God into Christian service, and I'm saying that your body is the temple of the Holy Ghost who is in you! That means your physical body is a sacred place, for it is looked upon as the abode of God. If God dwells in you, then you need to give some attention to that physical body.

If this concept of the presence of the Holy Spirit could ever impress itself upon God's people, we'd have no difficulty in evangelizing the world for Christ in our generation. If that's our calling, we've been called to be temples of the living God. That affects—

Conduct.

If your body is the temple of the Holy Spirit, how should you think? How should you act? How should you talk?

It never ceases to amaze me how people talk when they don't know who I am. I had that experience recently coming into Dallas from New Orleans. The plane was crowded, every seat taken. The man who sat in the middle seat, I was next to the aisle, was one of those who has been aptly described as having been vaccinated with a Gramophone needle and was still talking. He was one of these "wheelers and dealers" from Dallas, and before the trip was over we had a pretty good idea of what his annual income was and all the things he had going for him. But you should have heard his vocabulary! It wasn't very large, but it was spicy. I was sitting there wondering, yet knowing what his reaction would be when he found out who I was. I knew it would only be a matter of time until he would ask.

And after a period of time he did pause long enough to look at me and ask, "Who are you with?" I thought for a minute and said, "Well, that could be answered in a variety of ways, but basically I'm with the Lord." And he looked again and said, "What do you mean?" I answered, "Friend, I'm a Baptist preacher." About that time he grabbed his head, looked down and then looked around, shaking his head. The fellow next to the window was in on it by that time and he was smiling broadly. The man in the middle finally said, "There is only one thing that I can think of that would have been worse than this." I asked, "What's that?" And he replied, "For you to have played golf with me." Now, I don't know what kind of language he used on the golf course, but I know this! I know the vocabulary of a Christian ought to be ordered on the basis of the fact that the Holy Spirit lives within us. We ought not to say anything he would not approve.

In reality, my being a Baptist preacher ought not to have affected the language of that man. He doesn't owe me anything. I'm not his judge and he won't stand before me in the final day. But he ought to be reminded over and over that the Holy Spirit heard every word he said and that the Holy Spirit is the one to whom the apology should be made.

Does the presence of the Holy Spirit in your life, as a true believer, make a difference in the way you talk, the vocabulary that you use, the way you think, and the way you act?

Most of the religious questions that come to me concern themselves with certain activities. People ask me whether or not they should participate in various things. I'm asked to make judgments on matters that run from Sunday movies, to X- and R-rated shows, Sunday ball games, playing cards for prizes, going to dances, drinking a can of beer or cocktail, and on and on. Almost without exception the question comes to me like this, "Well, Preacher, which is *worst* for me to do . . . ?" and then the equation is posed.

There is a quick and final determination that can be made for all these problems that arise concerning Christian conduct. You don't have to come to me with it. You don't have to ask me what I think. What I think doesn't make a whole lot of difference. The Holy Spirit dwells in you and he'll lead you. Don't ever ask him which is *worse,* ask him what's *best* for you, for the kingdom of God, for your witness, and for Christ and other people. Ask him, "Lord, what wilt thou have me to do?"

Ask him about dancing and drinking, your Sunday night activities and matters of this kind, and if the Holy Spirit says okay, then you go right ahead. Proceed without any hesitance. But if the Holy Spirit does not give you a green light, cease and desist. You can't leave him behind, so if he tells you not to go and you go anyhow, you're taking him along because your body is his temple. He is in you and you're going to subject him to everything you're subjected to. You ought to know that you are in the presence of spotless holiness every day you live and every move that you make.

There's another area that needs to be covered. What about our self-imposed abuse of God's temple? Too many of us are guilty of intemperate eating habits and dig our graves with our teeth. We ought to be mindful of that and understand that our bodies are the temples of the Holy Spirit.

Others among us suck cancerous smoke into their lungs during every waking hour and seem to be totally oblivious to the findings of medical science. Listen you, your body is the temple of the Holy Spirit and if you, by your own self-imposition, weaken, debilitate your body and shorten your life by five or ten years, then you've robbed God. You have no right to rob God.

But on the other hand, if you can turn from some of these habits that detract from the vitality and health of this body, then, under God, you need to do it. I don't know of anything more incongruous than to find a medical doctor who is a habitual user of tobacco. Such a man preaches a doctrine that he does not really believe, for if he believed it he himself would be done with that which debilitates his physical body.

There are others among us who abuse the temple of God by working too many hours and by resting too few hours. Some of you appear to think that it's a test of spirituality to work without ceasing, to refuse to take a vacation, and to spend little or no time with your family. That's not only unchristian, but it is a denial of the Christ whom you follow. Many times during his earthly ministry he felt the need to separate himself from his immediate, pressing needs and to secret himself in solitude for prayer and restoration. If Jesus needed this, so do you and so do I.

The human body is amazingly resilient, yet the Christian is under the highest imaginable obligation to tidy up the temple, to keep it presentable, and to keep it usable for the glory of God. He dwells in you.

I don't have a catalog of do's and don'ts that I can pass out promiscuously, or give you a guideline of what you ought to do and how you ought to do it, but I do have one suggestion that I can make. Always keep in mind that the Spirit of God is in you eternally.

Dr. J. B. Gambrell, a giant among Baptists in Texas in earlier days, would frequently ask his wife if a certain shirt collar was too dirty to wear a second time. Mrs. Gambrell would always respond in the same way. Her answer was, "If there is any doubt about it, don't wear it."

That's an excellent criterion by which a Christian can regulate his daily conduct. If there is any doubt about a certain thing, if you wonder whether or not that would bring honor to Christ, then the very doubts about it ought to lead you to leave it alone and to do only those things that the Holy Spirit makes you feel good about and makes you know are in the will and purpose of God.

The Holy Spirit is in you. Let's live knowing that we are in the presence of our God every minute of every day.

4. The Spirit's Pervasion
MATTHEW 3:11

A great deal has been said and written about the decadent state of the church in our generation. Some otherwise erudite scholars have labeled ours the "post-Christian era" of human history. This, of course, implies that the age of the Christian faith and the church has passed, that we've outgrown these and there is no longer any need for them. It's not my purpose today to analytically categorize the faults and foibles of the church, although I know most of them, for I live with them day by day.

I don't think that the weaknesses of the church are necessarily to our shame, but perhaps to our credit. The church is not composed of perfect people. A saint is not a perfect person. The saints of the Lord who compose the fellowship of New Testament churches are people just like you and me. No one of us would claim to be perfect, so when you put this amount of imperfection together, even though dedicated to a common cause, the inevitable result is imperfection in our efforts to accomplish those goals.

I am not unduly concerned about the weaknesses and the glaring errors made by the church in the Kingdom. I'm only concerned when we, in our blindness, remain lethargic and become unwilling to change and unwilling to move. There is absolutely nothing wrong with failure unless or until it becomes a way of life. Failure is inevitable in the life of every human being. It's inevitable in the life of a church, but it should never become our standard and we should never become content with failure.

Every weakness to which you can point in the church today is a direct result of a lack of dependence upon the power of the Holy

Spirit. The truth is, if we are open to his leadership, if we are motivated and empowered by his presence, we would not fail! Our failures, then, ought to humble us. They ought to make us see ourselves more clearly and these same failures ought to require us to commit ourselves more totally to Christ and the fullness of the power of his Holy Spirit.

You won't learn much about first-century Christians unless you also learn their dependence upon the Holy Spirit. Any successes they had, any victories they achieved, came as a result of the presence and the power of God's Holy Spirit.

In the New Testament, in the Gospels, in Acts, and in the Epistles, there is a phrase found that has been widely used and widely abused. That phrase is: "filled with the Spirit." If I were to ask you what this phrase means, what would your response be? What would you say it means to be "filled with the Holy Spirit?"

This phrase appears five times in the book of Acts, three times in the Gospel of Luke, and one time in the book of Ephesians. Nine different times the New Testament refers to being "filled with the Spirit." I believe we do well to look at some of these in an effort to determine the context in which the filling of the Holy Spirit took place. I'm convinced that when we meet God's conditions, we, like the New Testament apostles, will also be filled with the Spirit. The first experience we'll call—

Possession.

It's found in Acts 2:4. This is the possession of the Holy Spirit that resulted in the filling, or being filled, or being pervaded by the Holy Spirit. The verse says, "And they were all filled with the Holy Ghost, and began to speak with other tongues, as the Spirit gave them utterance." This is not an unknown tongue. This is other languages. They spoke so that all the strangers gathered from over the known world in Jerusalem for the observance of the Feast of the Passover could hear in their native tongue and understand the gospel of Christ. The apostles, ignorant and unlearned men, received this spectacular and unusual gift of the Spirit by which they were given command of a foreign language for the purpose of proclaiming the gospel and honoring Jesus Christ.

Now let me underscore this. The phrase "filled with the Spirit" appears in this one instance only in connection with tongues, and this is not an unknown tongue, but known tongues. It was other languages. Now those who make the filling of the Spirit synonymous with speaking in an unknown tongue are revealing an ignorance of the truths of the Word of God. To be filled with the Spirit does not require a bizarre manifestation, a marginal expression of your faith such as speaking in an unknown tongue.

Up until the time of the coming of Christ, God had been *above* his people. He had revealed himself to them directly. With the coming of Christ, God was *with* his people, but after the ascension of Christ, on the day of Pentecost with the coming of the Holy Spirit, from that moment until the time of the second coming of Christ, God is *in* his people.

We read in the Old Testament the account of God's revelation of himself to his people when he was above them. We read in the New Testament the account of God's revelation of himself in Jesus Christ when he was with human beings. In keeping with the words spoken by Jesus our Lord, it was expedient for him to go away, for when he went away he sent another Comforter, even the Spirit of truth, for us today. This Holy Spirit is Christ living in the life of a believer. Christ dwells in the heart of the true Christian and his residence is never, never broken. He is the dynamic within the heart of the child of God who gives victory and authority to the Christian. Paul called this the "in Christ" relationship. He wrote, "Christ in you, the hope of glory." At the moment of conversion the Holy Spirit comes in. He is Christ in Spirit. Christ dwells within us. We refer to him as the Holy Spirit, but the task of the Holy Spirit is to magnify Jesus Christ. Jesus said this. He said when the Holy Spirit was come, it would be his responsibility to call to our remembrance everything Jesus had done and said.

Oftentimes in marginal expressions of faith, persons give the ascendancy to the Holy Spirit. They worship the Holy Spirit. They pray to the Holy Spirit. We are without authority to do that. We're not to pray to the Holy Spirit. We're not to exalt him. We're to exalt Jesus the Christ. Now he is present in the heart of the believer, yet his presence does not signify possession. He can only possess a believer when the believer surrenders his life to him.

How can you do that? You can only do it in one way, that is, by opening up every area of your life to his direction. That has to do with your occupation. Are you working where Christ wants you? Are you occupying yourself with a job that is Christ honoring? Open up your life in that regard and pray sincerely and openly "not my will but Thine be done." Be willing to occupy yourself with any position he leads you to fill.

This has to do also with your choice of life's partner. You have to be open to his leadership in coming to the marriage altar to be joined together in the indissoluble bonds of undying love.

You must be open to the direction of God's Spirit and his leadership in your social life. There are some places Christians ought not to be seen. There are some activities in which Christians ought not to take part. How can you know? You can only know when you open up your social life to his leadership. This is the openness that results in the possession of the Spirit. He possesses those areas of your life which you give to him and he cannot possess them until you give them.

During the ten days of praying prior to Pentecost, the Holy Spirit got possession of the Christians. He was already present in their hearts. He came in when they were saved, but he got possession of them. He even controlled their minds and their lips. I don't imagine they used many four-letter words, or the equivalent to four-letter words in the Greek language, when they were proclaiming the gospel. I can imagine that the Holy Spirit cleaned up their vocabulary. I believe the Holy Spirit controlled their minds when he gave them the ability to speak in a language that was not their native tongue. So the Spirit took possession of these Christians as they prayed during the days preceding Pentecost.

It's interesting, now, to note the results of the possession of the Holy Spirit. When he possessed these 120 believers, the result was Jesus Christ was exalted and the lost were saved by the thousands. I'm submitting to you, on the authority of the Word of God, that the possession of the Holy Spirit today will result in the same thing.

I'm also reminding you that God has given us the prerogative of evaluating fruits. "By their fruits ye shall know them." What are you to say about these who, with glib tongues, claim to be Spirit-filled and Spirit-empowered who have absolutely no fruits to show for Spirit possession? They may be possessed by some spirit other than the Holy Spirit, for when the Holy Spirit possesses a believer the result is the exaltation of Jesus Christ and the salvation of lost persons.

Sometimes perhaps we might be accused by the unknowing of being polytheists. Maybe someone not familiar with the Christian faith would say, "These people are worshipping three gods, God the Father, God the Son, and God the Holy Spirit." Such an idea is in gross error, for God is one, though he chooses to manifest himself in three distinct ways. I am looking at one hand, but that one hand is composed of five fingers. These fingers can operate separately or they can operate as a unit. So it is with God. He can choose to manifest himself separately or he can manifest himself as One Being. When we are filled with the presence and power of God's Spirit, that's positive proof that he possesses us, that every area of life has been open to his scrutiny and direction.

Let's take another of these passages. This one in Acts 4:8 points to—

Performance.

"Then Peter, filled with the Holy Ghost, said unto them." There follows here in the fourth chapter of Acts the sermon Peter preached when he was asked a question. The question was "by what name or by what power" he had healed an impotent man. This cripple had been gloriously restored to full health. The people were curious. "By what name or by what power have you performed this miracle of healing." The apostle Peter told them in no uncertain terms.

The Pentecostal transformation of the apostles is amazing to behold. Read of their lives prior to Pentecost and you find that from the time of the crucifixion and ascension until the day of Pentecost, they were a frightened group of people. They were so afraid they stayed primarily behind closed doors. They weren't out witnessing boldly, for they were not even certain themselves that Christ was yet alive. After the Pentecostal experience they were so completely changed that these once fearful persons stood in the presence of leaders of religion and government and openly defied them. They stood in the presence of a magistrate who had commanded them to quit preaching and teaching in the name of Jesus, looked him in the eye and said, "We must obey God and not you." You can imagine the raw courage that this required, most especially when they knew that their lives could be exacted for defiance of established authority. The secret of that boldness was the possession of God's Holy Spirit.

We find a prayer in Acts 4:29–30 which these apostles prayed. Underscore that prayer. Their prayer was exactly the prayer we ought to be praying every day. They prayed for "boldness!"

If I were to be asked the prime need for our church in this hour, I believe I'd be forced to conclude that our greatest need is the need for boldness on the part of members of this church in sharing their faith. If we are to possess that boldness it will come only when the Spirit of God possesses us.

Honestly now, don't you cringe a little on the inside when opportunities for witness come your way? Don't you look for and usually find an excuse to keep from saying a good word for Christ and his kingdom? Chances are most of us are indicted by questions like that, for the truth is we do not possess the holy boldness that is one result of the possession of the Holy Spirit. The Holy Spirit makes us bold in telling the world what we know about Jesus Christ.

Every Christian has open doors for witnessing. You have opportunities for witnessing that I do not have. There are persons in your circle of acquaintances who are unknown to me. Every day, everywhere you go, you have the privilege and opportunity of sharing your faith. How often we let these opportunities slip through our fingers!

I'm convinced that most church members really do know Jesus Christ. I'm convinced most of us have had an experience of conversion at the hands of Jesus Christ. But I'm also convinced that our greatest lack is the lack of this boldness that would make us unashamed witnesses for the Lord Jesus.

Have you ever wondered at the ability of some other person whom you know to say the right word at the right time? To share his faith in a winsome, attractive way that doesn't offend, but magnetizes? Have you wondered about that? Then, friend, wonder no more. That's a gift the Holy Spirit gives us when he possesses the life of a believer. He'll give you that gift if you'll give him all that you have. What he gives you is the best and he'll give you his best when you give him your best. The requirement is to dethrone self and enthrone Christ.

The apostle Peter on the day of Pentecost had no more access to the Holy Spirit than you or I. He had no greater measure of the Spirit's power than is available to you and me. What I'm saying is you can be Spirit-filled and Spirit-empowered and exalt Jesus Christ and bring others to know him when you meet God's conditions. You don't have to be ordained to be Spirit-filled. You don't have to be a deacon to be Spirit-filled. You don't have to be a leader in the Sunday School or an officer or worker in the Training Union. You don't have to be anything except submissive, and if you're a child of God and open your life to his direction, he'll give you holy boldness.

Let's take a look at one more of the phrases. This one we'll call—

Pronouncement.

It's found in Acts 13:9, "Then Saul, (who is also called Paul,) filled with the Holy Ghost. . . ." Whatever else your thoughts concerning Paul may include, you certainly must add the fact that he was no sissy. There was no evidence of cowardice in the life of this man and he knew nothing of the curse of peaceful coexistence with sin. Paul, like our Lord, could not live in the presence of flagrant sin.

At the time of this text, Acts 13:9, Paul and Barnabas were invited to appear before a deputy of the island of Paphos, Sergius Paulus by name, and share their faith. They were delighted to do so. They were on a missionary journey. This was the thing that they were committed to, but when they came to tell Sergius Paulus about Christ and the Christian faith, there was a heckler in the crowd. This man was a sorcerer, or magician. His name was Elymas. All the time Paul and Barnabas were trying to tell Sergius Paulus what it meant to be a Christian, Elymas was standing over to the side, maybe close to them, possibly shouting obscenities, maybe laughing and ridiculing them, maybe trying to stir up the animosity of the crowd around them, seeking in every way to prevent their proclamation of the gospel. You'll recall Paul's pronouncement. He exposed this man. He "read his title clear" and said to him face to face, "O full of all subtlety and mischief, thou child of the devil, thou enemy of all righteousness, wilt thou not cease to pervert the ways of the Lord?"

Paul wasn't trying to create a favorable public image. He wasn't interested in how this would affect those who heard him. He wasn't concerned with how they'd react to that pronouncement. He had one overriding concern: he was concerned with what Christ thought, and in light of that he could not have cared less what anyone else thought.

This was not really the way to curry favor. He had not read Dale

Carnegie's books and knew little about how to win friends and influence people for worldly purposes. The only one he was trying to befriend, the only one he was trying to please was Jesus Christ.

When followers of Christ wink at sin, when we remain tongue-tied in the presence of evil, when we get more concerned about what people think than about what God thinks, then it is quickly apparent that we are not filled with the Holy Spirit. A Spirit-filled Christian will know sin when he sees it and will not live in peaceful coexistence with it.

Paul's pronouncement ought to be heard more frequently in our day and generation. We need to be open-eyed to evil of every kind, and though we speak the message of God's judgment, it ought to be a message spoken in love and with an appeal for those who are guilty of violating God's law to turn from sin and receive God's forgiveness through receiving Jesus Christ.

Many years ago in Australia, at the conclusion of an evangelistic service conducted by Dr. R. A. Torrey, a man with the physique of a prizefighter came up to the evangelist. He looked at him with indignation in his eyes and wrath in his voice and said: "I am not a Christian, but I am moral, I am upright, I am honorable, and I am blameless. I want to know, Dr. Torrey, what you have against me?" Being faced with a person so obviously superior in physical strength would have caused most men to quake and tremble. Yet Torrey, in the boldness, the strength, the power, the courage of the Holy Spirit, looked him straight in the eye and said, "Sir, I charge you with high treason against heaven's King."

That ought to be the uncompromising pronouncement of every Spirit-filled Christian to every lost person in all the world. Those who have rejected Jesus Christ are guilty of high treason against heaven's King.

That's the pronouncement stated to all who are lost. You're guilty of high treason against heaven's King. But the pronouncement is made with the prayer that you'll turn from sin and receive Jesus Christ, God's greatest gift, in whom is eternal life.

5. The Spirit's Possession
2 CORINTHIANS 5:17

In this effort to expound the doctrine of the Holy Spirit, we've emphasized basic truth that is known to most Christians, but which somehow has been allowed to become a little bit fuzzy in the minds of many.

We have underscored the truth that we do not "get" the Holy Spirit so much as he "gets" us. It's not the effort of a Christian to possess the Spirit. The effort of a true Christian is to allow the Spirit to possess him. If we were to possess the Spirit, we could possibly have the same attitude revealed in the lives of various men in New Testament times who wanted the power the apostles displayed in order to magnify their own causes. We could become egocentric about it if the ultimate in Christian living was to possess the Holy Spirit. There is no room for egocentricity, or self-seeking, so it must be our purpose to let the Spirit get us. These are facts we have sought to reemphasize during this study.

We have pointed to the truth that the Holy Spirit is the agent of regeneration. You are not born again by your own power. You're not born again by your devotion to the things of the Spirit. You are born again by an act of God. It is a transforming, instantaneous, regenerative act by which we are given new natures. The very moment you repented of sin and asked Jesus Christ to come into your heart and live in your life, in that moment he made you a new creature. Old things passed away. In other words, God took his own divine eraser and erased everything in your past life of sin. He forgave it all. He put your sins behind him where he could see them no more. He separated you from your sins as far as the East

52

is from the West, and when God applied his divine eraser he came into your life and imparted to you a new nature.

There is a sense in which we are 100 percent dependent upon Jesus Christ. We're dependent upon him wholly for what he did *for* us on that skull-shaped hill called Calvary. God, in human form, became sin for us, even though he knew no sin, that we, who were dead in our trespasses and sins, might become the righteousness of God through him. We are wholly dependent upon what Jesus did for us at Calvary.

But there's another sense in which a Christian is wholly dependent upon the Holy Spirit. We are dependent upon what he does *in* us by the power of God imparting to us new natures. And so, in this sense, we are wholly dependent upon Christ and also wholly dependent upon the Holy Spirit. We simply cannot exist spiritually without the vicarious suffering, death, and sacrifice of Christ, nor can we live without the regenerative work of the Holy Spirit in our hearts.

I would like in this chapter to try to answer the simple question, Why must the Spirit possess us? Why is it necessary for the Holy Spirit to "get" us? I can give you a thumbnail answer in one sentence and then spend the rest of my time expounding that. The answer is: We must let the Holy Spirit possess us because we have sinful natures. We're corrupt, we've perverted, we've switched everything God intended, mixed it all up, jumbled it into a hopeless mess, and the only way it can ever be straightened out is by the power of God when he controls our lives.

Like Adam, we have the tendency to sin. Now we're not thieves stealing forbidden fruit like Adam and Eve, but we have identically the same tendency in our lives in that when we are left alone, we can't be trusted. Anytime we are left up to our own devices, by nature, we'll choose the shady, the evil, the wrong thing. In that sense we are like Adam.

We're not guilty of Adam's sin nor held responsible for the sin he committed. God only holds us responsible for our own sin, and that is a great enough burden of responsibility for anyone. We are like Adam in that anytime we have the opportunity to choose, we choose to sin rather than to do right. We are imperfect, we are corrupt, and God cannot overlook our imperfection and our corruption. That's why we have to become new creatures. That's why the Spirit must possess us to impart a new nature for us to be acceptable to God; and that, very simply, is what this chapter is all about.

In 2 Peter 1:3–4 we read: "According as his divine power hath given unto us all things that pertain unto life and godliness, through the knowledge of him that hath called us to glory and virtue." Now, get this sentence: "Whereby are given unto us exceeding great and precious promises: that by these ye might be partakers of the divine nature." How are we to partake of the divine natures? By the exceeding great and precious promises that are found in the Word of God!

This Scripture passage tells us two things. It tells us these promises are in the Word of God. If there is no other reason for you to be interested in Bible study, in learning and applying the truths of God, that one reason is foremost and sufficient. If there was no personal delight to be found in the study of the Word of God, this one reason is compelling. These exceeding great and precious promises are recorded in the Book. If you're indifferent to Bible study, if you think that's kid stuff, you had better go back and check your experience. The only way we can be partakers of the divine nature is through these exceeding great and precious promises.

The second truth found here is we are partakers of that divine nature. Now what are the results of the possession of the Holy Spirit? What comes about when the Spirit controls us?

In a recent youth service we asked the young people to give personal testimonies. One testimony came from a young man who had been witnessing to a friend at school. His friend at first was cold and unreceptive to the gospel, simply because he loved the sin he was committing. He didn't want to give it up. Do you have a certain sense of reluctance about giving yourself in totality to God? Are you afraid of what God might call on you to do? My friend, if you'll commit yourself in totality, if you'll surrender your life to him and pray for him to possess you, I can promise you the most exciting, the most joyful, zestful life your mind could ever imagine.

You don't deprive yourself to serve God. You add a dimension in life that you'll never discover in any other way. When the Spirit possesses us, he first of all gives a new—

Will.

In 1 Corinthians 2:14 we read: "The natural man receiveth not the things of the Spirit of God [the natural man is the unregenerate man, the lost man]: for they are foolishness unto him: neither can he know them, because they are spiritually discerned."

Have you ever wondered why a sinner doesn't wake up? Have you ever questioned why a lost person doesn't come to his senses? How can they be so foolish. Sometimes we've wanted to take such a person by the shoulders and shake him until he comes to a realization of fact instead of fancy.

Have you ever been appalled at the way some people live, with apparently no pang of conscience? I have wondered about that. I oftentimes wonder about that on Sunday when on the way to church. I see people on the streets of our city, or in their front yards, engaging in activities that indicate a complete oblivion to the things of the Spirit. Somehow or other there wells up in me a desire to stop and begin to preach the gospel. How can they be so foolish? I'm sure their reaction would be a rejection of the gospel, for they are not awakened to the things of the Spirit.

Is it strange that some people seem to thrive on church attendance and fellowship with the brethren while others apparently have no interest whatever in these things? The answer is found in this verse, 1 Corinthians 2:14. The natural man (the lost, unregenerate man) cannot understand. His mind is blinded by sin. Because of this, the lost man can read the Bible from cover to cover and never understand the Bible is speaking to his own need.

When I was a student in college, during the summertime I worked in a manufacturing plant in my hometown that produced tanks and boilers. As you might imagine, every kind of human being, spiritually speaking, was represented in that tank and boiler shop. It was pretty tough duty. One of my responsibilities was to flange cold steel with a twenty-pound sledge hammer. After eight hours of that in a day, I would go home tired. It certainly kept me out of mischief those summers, because I was too tired at night to leave the house. After supper I went to bed!

One of the men with whom I was associated was proud of the fact that he had read the Bible through fifteen or seventeen times, yet there was nothing about his testimony to indicate he had any familarity with the Word of God. He was probably the most profane man working in that area. When he talked about his own personal activities, the kind of life he lived, there was nothing about his life to indicate he had any grasp of spiritual truth. I could not understand that. This man had read the Bible from Genesis to the Revelation fifteen or seventeen times and yet he was profane, immoral, and laughed at spiritual things. How can it be? This verse explains it. The lost man, the unregenerate, the natural man cannot understand. His mind is blinded to spiritual truths until the Spirit of God gives that mind perception.

This is why a man may master all the definitive books in his chosen discipline, he may be looked upon as an authority in the field of English literature, sociology, languages, or mathematics, and be a total ignoramus in the realm of spiritual things.

Young persons sometimes don't grasp this. It becomes a problem for our college young people. They hear a brilliant professor speak with authority about the biological sciences, or in the field of philosophy, and when that same professor, who is eminently qualified in one area, one discipline, begins to speak about spiritual

matters, referring to religion as being antiquated, passé, and out-
moded, when he sneers and laughs at the church and church
people, some young people still consider that man an authority,
though he may be illiterate spiritually.

Only the Spirit of God can impart a new will which enables a
human being to grasp spiritual truths. I'm saying no one can speak
with authority in the spiritual realm unless he has been born again.
I'm saying one may hold an earned doctor's degree in any or many
different fields of learning and still be totally ignorant when it
comes to spiritual truth. I hope you understand that.

I earned my doctorate in Greek New Testament. You'd laugh
at me if I were to pose as an authority in the field of nuclear physics
because I have an earned doctorate in Greek New Testament. It
is just as foolish for the man with a Ph.D. in nuclear physics to
pose as an authority in spiritual matters unless or until that man
has had this experience called the new birth. It's only by that
experience that God can impart to a human being a new will. Only
that new will can grasp spiritual truth.

There is a second thing the Holy Spirit does for us when he
possesses us. He not only gives us a new will, but he gives us a
new—

Walk.

When we are dead in our trespasses and sin we love evil and the
things of the world. We love the vile, the unspeakable, the sinful.
Our text reminds us that if a man is "in Christ," he is a new
creature. Old things pass away, all things become new. It is an
instantaneous process by which we are born again, but it is a
lifelong process in which we grow in our likeness of Jesus Christ.

When the Spirit possesses us, day by day we lose our taste for
the things of sin. Any man among us, who knew he once was a
prodigal but has now come home to live a life pleasing the Father,
can bear testimony to this truth: old things pass away. God gives
us a new walk.

The apostle Paul put it like this: "The things I once hated I now love." When he was a lost man he hated the things of Christian faith. He persecuted Christians. At the time of his conversion he carried on his person documents that authorized him to persecute Christians on sight. He once hated the Christian faith, but after the coming of the Holy Spirit in regenerative power, he began to love the things he once hated and he began to hate the things he once loved.

Now is that peculiar to the apostle Paul or is that standard equipment for the Christian? It is standard equipment! That's not optional. If you've been born again, the love for sin dies out in your heart. Maybe not in an instant, but over a period of time, as you allow the Spirit of God to possess you more and more fully.

Some of you have a problem with cigarettes. Do you want to quit smoking? Do you hate that stinking, vile habit? Do you really want to quit? I can tell you how, and I could call on fifty or a hundred people I know to tell you it will work. Ask God to take away that taste from you and give you a new taste. Just commit your life to the Lord and say, "Lord, I don't want to do anything in my life that won't honor Thee." Ask him to take that taste from you.

Do you have a problem with booze? Do you hate yourself when you allow booze to get it's hold on you? Have you said to yourself, "I'd quit if I could but I can't!" Oh yes you can, but not by yourself.

A friend called me recently to tell me he was a victim of alcohol. He said: "I don't know why I do what I do. I have no explanation for it, but I know I don't want to continue to live in this way." There is good news for you, friend! Ask God to give you a new taste. Ask him to help you let your love for booze die out and give you new loves and a taste for something constructive and worthwhile. Ask God to give you a love for spiritual things greater than your love for golf, or fishing, or hunting, or bridge, or cocktail parties, or anything else in your life that has become your besetting sin.

Do you want to know what your relationship to God is? I can tell you how to find out. What is it that keeps you from serving him? What comes in to keep you from doing what you ought to be doing as a Christian? What is it that takes precedence over church attendance, service for the Lord, fellowship with the brethren, and public worship? Whatever it is, that's your god. That's what you really love, for when you sublimate your relationship to God for anything or anyone else, that's your true god. Find your ultimate allegiance and loyalty, and you'll find out exactly where you stand.

When the Holy Spirit possesses us, he gives us a new will, a new walk, and thank God, he gives us new—

Wants.

John 7:17 reveals these words from the lips of Jesus: "If any man will do his will, he shall know of the doctrine." In other words, you've got to want to. A man must want to do God's will, so when he gets concerned about pleasing God and not himself, then his program of spiritual growth will be on its way.

For the one who has been born again, there is nothing to compare with the joy that comes in doing the will of God. This abiding joy is ours when we put Jesus on the throne and self on the cross. That's what Jesus was talking about when he said, "If any man will come after me, let him deny himself." Put yourself on the cross, crucify self, sublimate self, and put Jesus on the throne. Through that program of self denial, you can grow in Christ day by day.

The one who has had this impartation of a new nature understands the spiritual significance of spiritual discipline. If you are one of those church members who has stumbled through life, doing only what you want to do, you've missed it. You're not in the right league. You're in a different ball park, for the one who follows Jesus, who has received this new impartation of life by the Holy Spirit, knows that there are some things which, because of the carry-over of the old nature, he'll not want to do, but he'll do them anyhow, knowing this is what is pleasing to God and in his own best interests.

How many of you have said, "Well, I just don't like Training Union. I just don't like prayer meeting." So what? You ought to love the things of God and if that love is not present, begin by your own discipline to do those things that you know honor Christ and he'll give you a love for them. It will happen every time in the power of God.

Regular Bible study and prayer is not some horrible burden to be borne. It's a blessing if the Spirit of God possesses you. Loyalty to the church services is not some chore, but a challenge and a blessing. Tithing and witnessing, in a definite planned program, is not something that will create misery in your heart, it's that which gives joy when the Spirit of God possesses you.

The Spirit has to possess us in order for us to be new creatures affectionally, intellectually, and volitionally. Those are just big words to say what I have already said. He gives you a new will, a new walk, and new wants.

So the big question is, have you been born again? That question ranks in first magnitude. If your answer is no, if you are honest enough to say, "I have never been born again and the Spirit of God has never possessed me," then I've got good news for you. You can undergo this transforming experience if you are willing to repent of your sins and ask God to do for you what you can never do for yourself.

There is one big requisite, and it is surrender. Yield your will to his, trust him to do the rest, and he'll do it.

6. The Spirit's Pursuit
MATTHEW 28:18-20

Jesus Christ and the Holy Spirit are identical in nature and in character. Just like two of the three sides of an equilateral triangle, they are identical in nature, but different in manifestation. Maybe we can take this illustration and apply it in such a way that it will give insight to our study.

A current of electricity properly applied to a bar of metal can transform it into a magnet. That which has been negative becomes positive. The electricity and the magnetism are the same identical power, yet they have different manifestations. One transforms the character of the steel from negative to positive and the other has to do with the influence that bar of steel has over material of like kind.

Just so, in the Christian experience, it is the blood of Jesus Christ, God's Son, that transforms the life, the character, the nature of a believer from negative to positive. It is by the life, death, burial, resurrection, and the promised return of Jesus Christ that we become "new" in character, "new" in status with God, but it is likewise by the indwelling power of the Holy Spirit that we come to have an influence over other human beings for the honor of Christ.

In one sense Jesus Christ and the Holy Spirit are identical, but their ministry has different manifestations. Jesus Christ is the one who does a work *for* us, while the Holy Spirit is the one who does the work *through* us and *in* us. By faith in Jesus Christ we are afforded a new status before God. We're justified, we're made acceptable to him, but it is by the energizing presence of the Holy

Spirit that we come to have an influence among men for Jesus Christ. This Spirit-filled life is the normal, basic Christian life. So many of us have lived so long as a subnormal plane spiritually, that if we become spiritually normal the world would think we are abnormal.

How many times have you described someone else as a spiritual fanatic? How many times have you said in a deriding, derogatory tone: "He's just gone overboard on the subject of religion." The truth of the matter is that the person to whom you referred probably was living more closely to the New Testament pattern than you or I. Normal Christian living, everyday is Spirit-filled living. That's the life and testimony that has an influence and a magnetism in the lives of other people, drawing them to the Lord Jesus Christ.

We see the pursuit of the Holy Spirit in the work of evangelism. Probably this subject was suggested by that shockingly beautiful phrase of Francis Thompson, who referred to God as "the hound of Heaven," pursuing human beings down through the ways of time. God is like the hound on a trail who never quits until he finds his object. We can see the pursuit of the Holy Spirit, first of all, in—

Seeking.

The Holy Spirit loves men. He is able to penetrate the debris of sin in the life of every human being and to find in us that image of the most high God, however horribly defaced that image may be. He's the one who can see beyond the obvious, the superficial, the external. He's the one who can discern the very being of a human and he sees in us something altogether lovely and beautiful for which God sent his only begotten Son into the world, to die that we might live. The Holy Spirit is the one who loves men and discerns within us something that is wonderfully potential.

We remember Jesus weeping over the sin of the spiritually hardened Jerusalemites. The grief of Jesus Christ is the grief of the Holy Spirit, for it grieves the Spirit of God not only when a child of God falls into sin, but it grieves the Spirit when the lost man turns from God to the devil, from heaven to hell, from salvation to everlasting damnation. The grief revealed in Jesus when he wept over sin is the grief of the Holy Spirit today when he sees us turning our backs upon God and the appeal to spiritual, Christian living. The Holy Spirit loves men. He's seeking today.

The Holy Spirit reveals Jesus Christ. You remember from history that in 1814 the British attacked Baltimore. Francis Scott Key, under a flag of truce, went on an errand to the British fleet. He was detained on board ship while the bombardment continued. Throughout the night, Key did not sleep. He stood on board the ship all night trying to pierce the darkness with his eyesight. He strained his eyes to see if he could tell whether or not "Old Glory" still flew. It was only when the rays of dawn broke that he was able to see the flag still proudly flying. That experience prompted him to write the words of our beloved song, "O, say can you see by the dawn's early light, what so proudly we hailed at the twilight's last gleaming?"

In that same fashion it is the Holy Spirit who brings the light of God to the mind of a human being, enabling one to see and understand the truths of God. No man will ever be able to understand how Jesus Christ, one Man, could die for all men. No man, save by the power of the Holy Spirit, can understand his personal need for salvation. It is the Spirit who reveals Christ. It is he who makes us know our needs.

The work of the Holy Spirit in seeking goes another step. The Holy Spirit reveals sin. No one can understand his need of a Savior until he understands that he's under the judgment of God, guilty and condemned before God. This isn't something we can transmit by human words, no matter how verbose or articulate we may be. No one of us can convict another human being of his need for a Savior. Only the Holy Spirit of God can perform that work.

Here's a pupil in school. He's trying desperately to work a math problem. He just cannot understand the procedure for solving the problem. The teacher, walking up and down the aisles observing the work of the pupils, stops and looks over the shoulder of that pupil. With her finger on the page, she points and asks, "What about this?" Then the pupil takes his pencil and begins to write. He slows down and as the teacher stands there she says: "Now, why not do this?" Again the pupil begins to write, and the problem starts to come into focus. Then suddenly he pauses again as the teacher says, "Now, you're ready to do this." Finally, with a look of triumph in his eyes, he faces her and says: "Oh, now I understand." The problem has not been simplified. It's not been changed. But the problem has been seen in its proper light. It's been grasped in perspective and then the solution comes.

One can never understand the efficacy of the blood of Jesus Christ shed for the sins of mankind until the Holy Spirit reveals that efficacy. The problem of sin is not simplified nor changed, but we can see it correctly along with its solution. So in the work of the Holy Spirit pursuing men, he makes us see the relevancy of God's way of redemption.

The Spirit's pursuit is seen in another step. We also see him in—

Sending.

This sounds almost unbelievable, but one of the things the Holy Spirit did prior to the day of Pentecost was to break up a prayer meeting. Do you recall the sequence in Acts? This is all the proof I need that God wants us to do more than just pray. Certainly God wants us to pray. We're urged to pray fervently. We're urged to pray ceaselessly. Jesus said men ought always to pray and not to faint. But that's not the end. There's more that you and I can do after we have prayed, for when the Holy Spirit got possession of the church prior to Pentecost, He broke up that prayer meeting and sent the congregation out into the streets, witnessing to the grace of God through Jesus Christ in redemption.

I believe if the Holy Spirit took possession of all churches across

America today, this would be precisely the procedure he'd follow. I believe he'd break up some of our worship services and prayer meetings and send us out where need exists.

The apostles, who were leaders in the church, as well as the multitude of the believers, who were the ordinary church members, were all sent out under the impulse of the Pentecostal possession of the Spirit of God to witness to their faith. They went out into the streets where people gathered, where men sinned and sorrowed and suffered, where humans were groping in the blindness of their despair and unbelief. There they proclaimed the good news: "There is hope for you. The good news is Jesus loves you, whoever you are, however dirty you may be, however broke you are, whatever your status in life, no matter what your educational background is, regardless of your bank account, God loves you!" They went all over the city of Jerusalem with that message, and thousands were saved.

After breaking up the prayer meeting, the record of which is found in Acts 1 and 2, the time came when the Holy Spirit had to break up the church and send out witnesses all over the known world. They came to the same point in time to which we have come. They enjoyed their fellowship so much and were so content with what they had and what they were, that they ceased to do the job Jesus commissioned them to do.

I would say this is one of the real dangers facing our church. We've got the sweetest fellowship this side of heaven. There's nowhere on the face of the earth I'd rather be than in a worship service with our congregation. Most of our people feel the same way, but it can be dangerous when we allow fellowship to become an end in itself.

Persecution came in the first century, the church was broken up, it ceased to meet together as a church and Acts 8:4 tells us what happened. "Therefore they that were scattered abroad went every where preaching the word." The Holy Spirit had to reveal that there was more for them to do than just to enjoy fellowship with each other, though fellowship was important.

God forbid that America will have to be overrun by Communism and the doors of our churches closed and locked before we begin to do what God wants us to do in our world! That may come.

Probably the most dynamic Christian witness being given today is the witness of those believers behind the Iron Curtain who are witnessing to their faith, even at peril of their lives. For the most part their churches are closed but they understand the gospel and are spreading the Word and telling the good news on a person-to-person basis. They don't have the advantages of television and radio over which to broadcast and telecast their services. They can't preach the gospel through the mass media, so they have to share it on a one-to-one basis. God forbid that churches will have to be closed in the land of the free and home of the brave.

The Holy Spirit, sending God's people to do God's work, stepped in next to break down the barriers of prejudice. This was racial and religious prejudice. It was Jew-Gentile prejudice. It was Jewish-Christian prejudice, for the Jews who were the first followers of Christ, came to the point where they insisted that for one to be a Christian he had to first become a Jew. They were so prejudiced against non-Jews that they were insisting that for one to be saved he had to become a Jew before he could become a Christian. The prejudice between Jew and Gentile was in every way comparable to the prejudices today we find between white man and black man, black man and white man, white and black people toward yellow people or brown people or red people. It was these barriers that the Spirit of God had to fragment in order to get God's people doing their job in their world.

Simon Peter, very unwillingly, went down to the home of a Gentile to share his faith. To his utter amazement a great revival broke out when he, a Jew, was willing to preach to Gentiles.

Philip learned that the gospel leaped across racial barriers, for when Philip was willing to sit down on a seat of a chariot with a black man and share his faith, the black man was saved and

Philip, the evangelist, had the opportunity of baptizing him.

The Holy Spirit is waiting to send us out, waiting on our surrender to his guidance. If we are to be sent, there is no room in our hearts for prejudice.

The pursuit of the Spirit is seen, finally, in—

Securing.

Aren't we grateful that we have the earnest, or the down payment, of the Holy Spirit in our hearts, witnessing to us that we do know him, whom to know aright means life everlasting!

Did you hear the story of the country preacher illustrating the security of the believer? He said: "You take a little baby and put him in a keg and seal it up. Then put the keg in a barrel and seal up the barrel. Take the barrel and put it in a hogshead and seal up the hogshead." And then he backed up and shouted, "Now this is what God does with his little babies, his babes in Christ. He takes them first and puts them in a keg and seals them up. That's the seal of the blood of Jesus Christ. Then he takes that keg and he puts it in a barrel and seals it up." He said, "That's the seal of the love of God the Father. Then He takes that barrel and puts it in a hogshead and he seals it up, and that," he said, "is the seal of the Holy Spirit." Then he added, "If the devil gets one of God's little babies, the devil's got to bust through that hogshead, bust through that barrel, and bust through that keg, and hallelujah, that's mo' bustin' than the devil can do!" Thank God for the security that is imparted to our hearts by the presence and power of the Holy Spirit.

A passionless ministry will never arouse a cold church and a cold church will never win a lost world for Jesus Christ. The Holy Spirit must warm our hearts and send us out to pass on that warmth to all with whom we come in contact.

From coast to coast, our nation is under a visitation of divine power. There's a deep hunger for spiritual truth found in this nation unlike anything we have ever seen or known. As always, the devil counters with extremism or with a bootleg, counterfeit brand of gospel.

In America today God is using some churches to reveal sane, scriptural, Spirit-filled evangelism. With all the conviction of my heart I believe our church is one of the churches God is using in that way.

Salvation by grace through faith does three things. First it is a work for us, then a work in us, and finally a work through us. For us, it is the work of redemption through the blood of Jesus Christ. In us, it is the work of sanctification by the work of the Spirit of God. Through us, it is the work of Spirit-motivated, Spirit-empowered evangelism. To be "in Christ" is to receive a new status, to be a participant in continued growth, and the producer of fruit for the honor of the Lord Jesus Christ.

Paul said, "There is therefore now no condemnation to them who are in Christ Jesus." Are you in him? If you are, he's done a work for you, he's doing a work in you, and he wants, more than anything, to do something through you. When the Spirit pursues you, it's for these purposes.

7. Test the Tongues
1 CORINTHIANS 12:13

Baptists are people of the Book. The statements of faith we have made across many centuries point out that the New Testament is our sole rule for faith and practice. That means it is our only authority. This implies that all valid spiritual activity must conform to the Bible, rightly divided.

No spiritual experience can be considered genuine or profitable unless that experience conforms to the infallible Word of God. Human experience does not require the conformity of the Book. The Book requires conformity of human experience. You cannot say, "Because this happened to me, the Bible must authenticate it." You must rather say, "The Bible says this, and if my experience does not conform to the teachings of the Bible, my experience is not a Christian experience nor is it valid spiritually." The Bible is the divine yardstick by which we measure all human experience.

I have known people to try to justify sin by saying, "This is God's will." I reject that. There's a Baptist preacher I knew at one time who, after an adulterous relationship with the wife of one of the members of his church, ran away with that woman, divorced his wife, and married the woman. He said, "This is God's will." That was a blatant lie. It is not God's will to violate God's commands. Any human experience you have that cannot be justified in the teachings of the Word of God is not a valid spiritual experience.

I assume you understand the magnitude of what I'm saying. You're not required to agree with me, but if you disagree I certainly would like to know what your authority is. No matter how ecstatic or frequent an experience one may claim with the Lord, if that experience is not biblically sanctioned and biblically grounded, it is spiritually spurious.

We're not saved on our own terms. We can't take some isolated experience that we have had and say, on the basis of it, "I'm saved." If we've been saved, we have been saved along the lines that God offers salvation and along no other lines. Every human being can't be saved the way he wants to be saved. He can't say, "This is what I would like to do in order to become a Christian," and count whatever experience he might choose as conversion. If you've not been converted along the lines of the teachings of the Word of God, then you cannot claim his salvation.

What is your personal final authority? Or in terms of the vernacular, what is your "hole" card? What's the final authority in your life? Is it what you think and feel, or is your final authority what the Bible teaches? Friend, don't be too quick to answer. This includes not just the matter of speaking in tongues, it also includes storehouse tithing, forgiving our enemies, turning the other cheek, and being willing to go the second mile. If your Bible is your final authority, you are not authorized to pick and choose the parts you'll believe and the parts you might wish to reject. If the Bible is your final authority, you must take it in totality and seek to apply it day by day in your witness.

Think first with me about the—

Context

—of the matter under discussion. The so-called charismatic movement now has worldwide proportions. It has affected Roman Catholics as well as Protestants.

In June of 1972, for instance, nearly 12,000 Roman Catholics gathered at Notre Dame, Indiana, for a charismatic conference. Not all of these spoke in tongues, but they were there because of their interest in the charismatic movement. This has been felt in the main-line denominations of Protestantism such as Baptists,

Methodists, Presbyterians, Episcopalians, and others.

One author has asserted that "between two and three million, and perhaps a great many more, Americans have had a strange, personal experience of religion known as speaking in tongues."

I took Strong's Concordance and looked for the word "tongue." In the singular it appears thirty-three times in the New Testament. In eight of these appearances it refers to an "unknown" tongue. The word "tongues" (plural) is found twenty-seven times in the New Testament, sixteen of which refer to the phenomenon under consideration. There is only one mention of tongues in the four Gospels and that's in a disputed passage referring not to an "unknown" tongue, but to a "new" tongue.

I'm saying the four New Testament books that give us primarily the biographical material from the life of Christ have no mention of the phenomenon. There is only one of the twenty-one Epistles of the New Testament that refers to speaking in an "unknown" tongue, or glossolalia, and that is 1 Corinthians. There is no mention of it found in the book of the Revelation, and Jesus Christ never commanded this nor did he participate in this activity.

This is a sketch of the context and brings us to the matter of—

Confusion.

We find it worldwide today on this subject.

At the outset let me state without equivocation that I do not reject the validity of this spiritual gift. I don't deny the spiritual gift known as "tongues." It is described in the pages of the New Testament as one of the gifts which the Holy Spirit gives. Now if the Bible is my sole rule of faith and practice, I don't have a right to reject the verses that say that this is a valid spiritual gift bestowed by the Holy Spirit.

I know some persons, Christian people, scholars, whose sincerity cannot be questioned who restrict glossolalia to the first century. They contend that it was a spiritual gift given for a specific moment in time and the purpose has already been fulfilled. I do not question their sincerity nor reject their right to their interpretation.

I know others who build a case for this phenomenon saying that it actually is the use of a foreign language unknown to those who hear it, but known by a certain nationality or group of people in the world. This is supported by the fact that in almost every instance, if not every instance, where there is a mention of "unknown" tongues in the King James, the word "unknown" is italicized. That means the italicized word is not in the original manuscript. Therefore some believe this present-day phenomenon is not New Testament, because New Testament glossolalia was a divine gift granting the ability for a person to speak in a language that he had never known, had never studied, but was given this gift by the power of God. Again, I do not question the sincerity of those who are thus convicted.

I believe, however, that the sovereign Spirit of God is able to bestow his gifts upon any person at any time and at any place in the world. I will not quench or limit the Holy Spirit by refusing him complete authority and freedom. I'm saying I believe the Holy Spirit can give this gift today.

Having said this, I must affirm that everywhere there is something genuine in the spiritual realm, the devil manufactures something counterfeit. That's his *modus operandi*. The devil does not seek to thwart the work of the Kingdom by direct head-on opposition nearly so much as he does by the manufacture of that which is counterfeit or spurious.

There is much historical evidence that glossolalia has never been limited to Christians. I'm saying that Christians are not the only ones who have spoken in unknown tongues. This is practiced by pagans, it is practiced by those involved in the occult, and it also has been practiced by some of those who are a part of the drug subculture of our society.

Persons who have come out of the drug culture have described experiences when they, under the influence of drugs, have spoken in an unknown tongue. It is precisely because of this that it is mandatory for you and me to "test the tongues" or to "try the spirits" as God's Word authorizes us to do. It is only in this way that we might be able to determine the real or genuine, from the counterfeit.

One Pentecostal author candidly faced these facts and acknowledged: "There is something radically wrong with the experience that gives you gifts and does not give you holiness." I believe he put his finger on the sore spot. If one's life does not measure up to the gifts he says God has given him, you have a right to put a question mark over such a one. Jesus authorized us to inspect fruit: "By their fruits ye shall know them."

Without question there are Christian people who have never spoken in tongues whose lives and Christian commitment match in every way the life and commitment of those who have spoken in tongues. I believe everyone would agree with that.

The test of a true prophet is whether or not his prophecies come to pass. In the Old Testament, when a man claimed to be a prophet, they tried him on the basis of whether or not his prophecies came to pass. "By their fruits ye shall know them."

What's the test of tongues? The basic test is holiness. It is the revelation of God's supreme gift, which is love. If a person claims to have a gift from God and it does not result in greater Christlikeness, then that gift which he claims is suspect. The test of a tongues-speaker is not his ability to speak in an unknown tongue, for even a pagan or a Hindu can do that, but the test is what he believes to be true about Jesus and whether or not he obeys the commands of our Lord. If you test the tongues, do it on the basis of God's Word and if tongues do not result in greater Christlikeness there is real reason to question the validity of that gift which is claimed.

Now think with me about—

Conversion.

It is a denial of the Bible to claim that salvation is always attended by speaking in tongues. It is a rejection of the teachings of the

Word of God to hold that the baptism of the Holy Spirit is always attested by glossolalia.

Conventions are held by certain groups across our nation in which they are praying for "the baptism." They might do well to pray for conversion, for if they have never received the baptism of the Holy Spirit, they are not saved. If they received the baptism of the Holy Spirit, it is not necessarily accompanied by speaking in tongues. Not a single Scripture that I have ever been able to find supports the contention that a believer is to seek baptism in, by, or with God's Spirit. My Bible doesn't tell me to seek this so-called "second blessing" which is called by some the baptism of the Holy Spirit.

In fact, in 1 Corinthians 12:30 Paul clearly indicates that glossolalia is not for everyone. Those who contend that the baptism of the Holy Spirit is always accompanied in speaking in tongues have closed their eyes to certain biblical truths.

Our text reminds us that by one Spirit we are all baptized in one body—by one Spirit we are all baptized. Does that mean that all of us speak in tongues? Not according to Paul in 1 Corinthians 12:30. The baptism of the Holy Spirit is an act of God that places a believer into the family of God and into the body of Christ, which is Christ's eternal church. There were many carnal Christians in that group to whom Paul wrote, and they didn't all speak in unknown tongues.

Dr. Jack Gray of Southwestern Seminary made this strong and pointed comment: "To have a great encounter with God and to come away enamored with the experience rather than with God is sophisticated idolatry. We are not to magnify the gift; we are to magnify the Giver of all the gifts. We are not to go out as an evangel of our gifts or of our experience, but we are to go out as an evangel for God."

Another contemporary theologian reminded us that people who demand a higher norm of truth than human experience are really asking for an idol. To sum this up, tongues cannot be the determining test of one's conversion. It is not biblical to equate the baptism of the Holy Spirit with glossolalia. Conversion comes in and through Jesus Christ, and is not dependent upon how to feel about it. Conversion is dependent upon the integrity of Almighty God. If we believe him, conversion comes on the basis of his promise, not on the basis of how we might feel about it. Human feelings have never been the test of a conversion experience.

If you've never found the joy that comes through God's faith and power, then you've missed life's highest joy. If you've never received the baptism of the Holy Spirit, this is tantamount to saying you've not been born into God's family, for in the moment of belief and faith God's Spirit brings about this work in us that makes us his and his forever. Through Christ, a Christian can sing:

> All the way my Saviour leads me;
>   What have I to ask beside?
> Can I doubt His tender mercy,
>   Who through life has been my guide?
> Heav'nly peace, divinest comfort,
>   Here by faith in Him to dwell!
> For I know whate'er befall me,
>   Jesus doeth all things well.

I'm not here to discuss an experience. I'm here to extol and exalt Jesus. He's the one who can save, he's the one who can empower, and he's the one who grants joy to the heart of the believer. If you don't know Jesus, he's alive, and more than anything else, he wants to live in your heart. He wants to transform your life, he wants to baptize you, to completely immerse you in his love, his joy, and his peace. Will you let him?

8. The Spirit Perverted
1 CORINTHIANS 14:33

This is a difficult subject because the matters with which we'll deal are those about which there is little agreement among denominations. I don't write vindictively nor denounce those whose denominational persuasion is different from my own. I rather come to share with you my interpretation of the Book, and I trust this interpretation, coming after a period of study and number of years of devoting my life to the Bible, will stand the test of exegesis and not eisegesis.

These two words are well known to Bible scholars. The word "exegesis" has the same prefix as the word "exit." You know what exit means: it means the way out. So exegesis means reading out of the Bible what the Bible is saying to us. "Eisegesis" is trying to read into the Bible what you might want the Bible to say. Eisegesis is a smirch on the integrity of scholarship and it's not to be indulged in by those who are intellectually honest. Exegesis is our purpose, for we are trying to reconstruct what Jesus is saying. He said it in a language different from our own. He spoke in Greek, though he probably was trilingual. He also likely had a command of Hebrew and Aramaic in addition to Greek.

What we have in the King James translation is just that. It's a translation of what was written in Greek, recording the words of Jesus. What I'm attempting is to give you my interpretation of what the Bible teaches from the standpoint of the original language and with consistency toward all of the other teachings in the Bible. I don't believe that Holy Scripture denies itself. I don't believe that Scripture teaches something here and over here it denies itself. I believe if there is an apparent discrepancy it's due to our lack of understanding. That which might seem to contradict something else is because of our improper grasp of one or the other of the passages. So what I shall write is an attempt to correlate the teachings of the Bible, not in some isolated verse or on the basis of one passage, but on the basis of the broad spectrum of the totality of the Word of God.

There are three basic areas in which I believe there is a misinterpretation of the Bible and a misunderstanding of the work of the Holy Spirit. These three areas have led and are leading to gross error. First, let's examine the matter of—

Sinlessness.

The persons who believe they are sinlessly perfect ordinarily refer to these verses in the First Epistle of John. This is 1 John 3:6–9. "Whosoever abideth in him [abideth in Jesus] sinneth not: whosoever sinneth hath not seen him, neither known him" (v. 6).

Friends, that's pretty pointed in the King James translation and it would lead, in this translation as we understand this language, to a belief in sinlessness. Verses 7–8: "Little children, let no man deceive you: he that doeth righteousness is righteous, even as he [Jesus] is righteous. He that committeth sin is of the devil; for the devil sinneth from the beginning. For this purpose the Son of God was manifested, that he might destroy the works of the devil." Here's verse 9: "Whosoever is born of God doth not commit sin; for his seed remaineth in him: and he cannot sin, because he is born of God." Now if you are a believer in the Bible, you read this in King James and quickly conclude this verse calls for sinless perfection. The King James translation, however, is an inadequate expression of the Greek tenses found here.

These are present tenses in Greek, and the present tense expresses linear action. The word linear is basically the word "line." You know what a line is. A line runs from a point at the left to another point at the right. The present tense in Greek expresses a line. The aorist tense in Greek, on the other hand, expresses point action, "doth not commit sin." These are present tenses in this text, expressing linear action or continuing action and that is the reason why Phillips' translation uses the word "habitually" to give adequate expression to this tense.

In verse 8 Phillips translates this: "The man whose life is habitually sinful is spiritually a son of the devil." That sin is a continuing practice, an unrelenting habit of one who is of the devil.

Williams, in his translation, expresses the Greek tense more adequately than does the King James Version when he defines it in this way: "No one who continues to live in union with Him [Jesus] practices sin; and no one born of God makes a practice of sinning." That's the tense and these both are better expressions of the Greek language. So, when we understand the true meaning, we come to realize that the Bible does not demand sinlessness on the part of a Christian. The Bible *does* say that a person who continues to wallow in the mire, the stench, the slime of sin, is revealing the fact that he has not ever been born again, for the person who has been born again, when he sins, is swept with remorse and cries out in contrition and confession.

We're not expected to be sinlessly perfect in this life, all of the other denominations that might teach this to the contrary notwithstanding. This is an indication, then, that the born again believer, the true Christian, does not continually, habitually violate God's law.

Another proof text used by persons in some denominations is found in the Gospel of Matthew, chapter 5, verse 48. "Be ye therefore perfect, even as your Father which is in heaven is perfect."

The word "perfect" in the King James translates a form of the Greek *telos*. It is the same word Jesus used on Calvary when he said, "It is finished." He was indicating completion. He was indicating well roundedness. The meaning of this Greek word far more nearly corresponds to our word "mature" than to the English word "perfect." Here again the Bible is not demanding sinless perfection as a test of one's Christianity. We are not required to be sinlessly perfect. It is stated that a Christian will not obviously, with a blasé attitude, habitually live in sin with no repentance and no sense of remorse. So Jesus is saying, "Be therefore mature, well rounded, finished, completed in your Christian faith" in so far as your commitment is concerned. If you are, though there are errors and sins and imperfections that will be obvious, no one will need to doubt your direction. No one will ever question whether or not you are really a Christian, but they'll know by your spirit of love and forgiveness that you are truly born of God.

This is one way that the Holy Spirit is perverted, by those who believe and teach that when we've got the Holy Spirit, we also have sinless perfection. In addition to sinlessness, let's look at another belief that has been perverted and that's the belief in—

Sanctification.

Sometimes this is equated with sinless perfection in the teachings of some denominations, but in most cases sanctification is looked upon as a second work of grace, something that occurs in the life of a Christian after he's been saved. They teach that you get saved at point X over here and at point Y over there you get sanctified, and that these are two separate, distinct experiences. Sanctification, oftentimes, is referred to as a second blessing. The vast majority of biblical scholars reject that view completely.

Dr. H. A. Ironside, one of the great preachers of a past generation, said: "To sanctify in the Christian sense is twofold, absolute and progressive." This I believe to be the teaching of the New Testament. Sanctification is an experience that takes place once and for all, yet it is a continuing experience measured by our growth in likeness of Christ.

If you will, just erase from your mind the word "sanctification" and substitute the word "Christlikeness." I believe they are synonymous. If we are being sanctified, we are becoming more and more like Jesus Christ. The Greek word *hagios*, from which the word "sanctification" comes, actually means holy. It means to set apart for God, something exclusively for his service. It's translated in many places holy, and in reference to the tithe the Old Testament uses a Hebrew synonym which says the tithe is holy unto God; set apart, something that's sanctified for God's use, not to be used for human purposes. It's for God's purposes, set apart. Sanctified means the same thing. When we are sanctified, we are set apart once and for all for God's service. That's the act we also call the new birth. That's the experience we call conversion. That's what we mean when we say, "I have been saved."

But we must also add that in the moment of our conversion, as Paul wrote, we are but babes in Christ. We're babies in our understanding. We're babies in our grasp of the Word of God. We're babies in our understanding of a Christian relationship with other people and in the application of the gospel to daily life. So we are being sanctified as we grow in knowledge, understanding, and likeness of the Lord Jesus Christ.

That's the reason, then, that all of us are saints. I still hear it. Hardly a week goes by that I don't hear it. People say, "Well, I'm not what you call a saint, but. . . ." What do you think a saint is? Do you think a saint is someone that the Roman Catholic church has canonized? That's what the Roman Catholics believe, but the New Testament teaches that a saint is a person who has been and is being sanctified. That means *you* are a saint. That's Saint Fred down here on the front row. Saint Melvin over there. And though I am a saint and though they are saints, we don't call one another "saint." The reason we don't is because the New Testament saints didn't call themselves saints.

Matthew never referred to Luke as Saint Luke. Luke never referred to the apostle Paul as Saint Paul. These designations we have in the King James translation, Saint Matthew, Saint Mark, Saint Luke, Saint John, are there as a direct result of the influence of Roman Catholicism on the translation of the King James. We don't refer to one another as saints. We don't even refer to these New Testament brothers in Christ as saints. We're all saints. We all have been sanctified, and by the grace of God, we are being sanctified. A saint is a human being in whom God has wrought his redemptive work, setting apart that human being for his use and for his glory. We don't refer to humans, dead or alive, as saints because they are no more saints than you and I.

Dr. E. Y. Mullins said: "In the New Testament the word sanctify has two meanings. To set apart to God's service, or belonging to God, and also, becoming inwardly holy." I think that's an excellent definition based on the teachings of the Word of God. For that reason everyone of us can say, if we have been saved: "I have been sanctified, and I am being sanctified. I've had the experience that set me apart in which God redeemed me from sin and made me his child, and now, in a process that's taking place daily and hourly, I'm trying to grow to be more like my Master." Growing in our likeness of Jesus is the process in which all of God's people are involved.

Then there's a third area in which the Spirit is perverted, and that's in the matter of—

Salvation.

These are the three, then, at which we are looking: sinlessness, sanctification, and salvation.

To say that salvation is incomplete until there is a second blessing or until one receives the "baptism," so-called, by which one speaks in an unknown tongue, is to deny the Word of God. Now I want to say that in love, but I'm prepared to stand and cover all the ground I'm standing on. If you'll get your Bibles I think we can find what the Bible says, upon which I base my very dogmatic statement.

The doctrine of justification, taught throughout the New Testament, is totally negated by the requirement of a second blessing or of an unknown tongue, or anything else! The entire Bible doctrine of justification is wiped out if you say that there has to be something in addition to the initial commitment whereby one becomes a child of God through God's redemptive work.

Look first at Romans 3:24–25. Verse 24: "Being justified freely by his grace through the redemption that is in Christ Jesus." We are justified by his grace, not by a second blessing, not by a so-called baptism involved in speaking in tongues. We are justified by his grace.

Verse 25: "Whom God hath set forth to be a propitiation through faith in his blood, to declare his righteousness for the remission of sins that are past, through the forbearance of God." That verse points out clearly that the sinner is justified by God's grace through the redemption that is in Christ Jesus.

Now, just as there are three persons in the Godhead, there are three aspects of justification. The first of these aspects is by grace, and that's the grace of God the Father. This person of the Godhead is actively involved in your redemption and mine. We are justified by grace. Look now, if you will, at Galatians 2:17. In this verse we read: "But if, while we seek to be justified by Christ, we ourselves also are found sinners, is therefore Christ the minister of sin?" This verse clearly says justification "by Christ." He's the second person of the Godhead and justification by Christ indicates that his life, his death, his burial, his resurrection satisfied the demands of God's righteous law in our behalf.

Now, back to Romans again. This time chapter 4, verse 5. "But to him that worketh not, but believeth on him that justifieth the ungodly, his faith is counted for righteousness." We are justified by faith. Our faith is counted or reckoned or imputed as righteousness. That simply says righteousness is outside the believer. It doesn't come because of how much you've given, it doesn't come because of how frequently you've attended: righteousness and justification are imputed by faith. Our faith is counted for righteousness.

How do we get righteous in God's sight? Not through our goodness, for we aren't. The only way we can be righteous before God is for him to impute, or count, our faith for righteousness. So we are justified by grace, that's God the Father; we're justified by Christ, that's God the Son; we're justified by faith, that's God the Holy Spirit who imputes, or counts, our faith as righteousness. All of this is to say, then, that salvation by grace through faith is a complete act, once and for all, by which one is justified. And if he's justified and stands reckoned to be just in the sight of God in the moment of his conversion, he doesn't need anything else to reckon him justified. This is a totally completed act. To add any additional requirements to this act of God is to bring into question the totality of Christ's power to redeem.

If you say one must have a second blessing or one must have a so-called "baptism" of the Holy Spirit accompanied by speaking in tongues in order to be saved, you have denied the Bible doctrine of justification and you have negated salvation by grace through faith alone.

In Galatians 3:2 the apostle Paul points out that one receives the Holy Spirit in the moment he believes. "This only would I learn of you, Received ye the Spirit by the works of the law, or by the hearing of faith?" Anyone who ever tries to teach you that you do not receive the Holy Spirit in the moment of your confession and your conversion denies the clear teaching of the Word of God. God's Spirit comes in fullness into the heart of the believer in the instant of salvation. There is no necessity for some additional second blessing, or so-called baptism and speaking in tongues, for one to be saved.

In Ephesians 1:13 the same truth is underscored. "In whom ye also trusted, after that ye heard the word of truth, the gospel of your salvation." Now get this, underscore it, mark it in your Book, and when some person who is misinformed or ignorant tries to tell you differently, read this verse of Scripture! ". . . in whom also after that ye believed, ye were sealed with that Holy Spirit of promise." When? When you got a second blessing? When you got some so-called baptism? No. "After that ye believed!" That's when you received the Holy Spirit. You may not have understood, at that moment, who he is or what he was capable of doing for you, but you received him. You received just as much of him as you were ready or willing to accept. So Ephesians 1:13 teaches that we receive the Holy Spirit in the instant of belief. He is not part of some "second" blessing. He is in the first blessing!

In the seventh chapter of the Gospel of John, read verses 38 and 39. "He that believeth on me, as the scripture hath said, out of his belly shall flow rivers of living water." Now what's that predicated on? The opening phrase, "He that believeth on me." Now get verse 39, "But this spake he of the Spirit, which they *that believe on him* should receive" (italics mine). The Holy Ghost was not yet given on the church. He was given on the church at Pentecost, yet every believer receives the Holy Spirit. In the moment you believed, you received God's Holy Spirit. God gives you all he has in the moment you give him all you have. When you turn your life over to him in totality, he makes available to you in totality everything he gives the Christian. It's all at your disposal. You may not understand the resources that are yours, you may not understand the fullness of that power, but it's yours and all that you have to do is claim it. All you have to do is to make yourself submissive and available and God endows you with power for the task you claim in his name.

The fact I want to underscore is just this: You may receive salvation and the full power of God's Holy Spirit right now. You don't have to wait for some future time. If you are already saved, the Spirit of the living God is resident within you and all you have to do to be Spirit-empowered is to let him lead you. Shift into neutral and let him take control and direct your life and use your lips, your voice, your ears, your mind, your hands, your feet, your business, your home, and your witness. All you have to do is to open your life to his direction. The fullness of his power can and will be yours in the very instant you want him to control you.

If you're not saved, the one step you must take is to repent of your sins and believe on the Lord Jesus Christ. If you repent of sin and turn from it and turn to Jesus Christ, I can guarantee you, on the basis of the authority of his word, he'll not turn you down. "Him that cometh unto me I will in no wise cast out."

I don't care what you've done. I don't care how deeply into sin you may have sunk. There's no sin Jesus cannot forgive except your sin of not letting him forgive. In the very moment you let him forgive you, when you turn from sin and accept what he's offering, in that moment God's Holy Spirit takes up residence in your life and he'll give you joy and peace such as you've never known in all your days.

9. The Spirit's Purpose
MATTHEW 3:11; ACTS 1:5

These verses of Scripture and others related to them have been misinterpreted in a number of ways in our time. There are a variety of interpretations, and though I believe there is room for some difference of opinion, I do not think we are at liberty to abuse the teachings of the Word of God. I do not believe a passage in Holy Writ teaches one thing in one place and in another place denies or refutes that which has been stated.

There may be passages in seeming contradiction, but when they are rightly understood, when we rightly divide the Word of Truth, when the Spirit of God reveals God's truth to our hearts, there is no contradiction. It's because of that conviction that I am writing on this subject.

Some denominations base their interpretation of the entire Bible and all Christian experience on these two verses in Matthew and Acts. Because of the extreme nature of classic Pentecostalism, the so-called Holiness churches, other denominations have tended to ignore the baptism of the Holy Spirit. We have shied away from it and don't discuss it.

If we go to one extreme it will lead us to become superficially fanatical. We don't want that, surely, but to go to the other extreme will leave us with a faith devoid of power for world conquest. I'm convinced that the proper approach to the doctrine of the baptism of the Holy Spirit is not at either extreme, but somewhere between the two. It's for that reason we're considering this subject and studying it in light of a number of other Scriptures.

It's humanly impossible to sum up the purpose of the Holy Spirit in any one chapter or series of treatises. Across the years of my ministry I probably have preached forty or fifty different sermons on the doctrine of the Holy Spirit. No one of these, nor all of them together, have exhausted the subject, because the subject is infinite. The Holy Spirit is infinite. No one of us can corner all the truth of him or his ministry.

Let's begin our investigation by pointing out what I judge to be—

Confusion.

Sign-seeking is an evidence of confusion. I base my statement on the teachings of Jesus Christ in Matthew 16:1. "The Pharisees also with the Saducees came, and tempting desired him that he would shew them a sign from heaven." These were the religious leaders, and on more than one occasion they asked Jesus for a sign. They wanted proof of the authenticity of Jesus Christ. May I remind you that Jesus labeled these sign-seekers a "wicked and adulterous generation." He flatly stated that they would have no sign given them except the sign of Jonah. When they came to Jesus saying, "We want proof of your authenticity," Jesus responded, "The only proof I'll give you is the sign of Jonah." Jonah, in some ways like Jesus, came preaching repentance to the people of Nineveh. He was possessed by no sign from heaven other than his message.

Jonah knew all about that whale, or great fish. I don't know for sure that it was a whale. The Bible doesn't say it was a whale, it says a great fish. Jonah knew all about that great fish and his experience, and the people of Nineveh didn't. He could have preached on his call and conversion, and the Lord's chastening rod. Yet when Jonah arrived in the city and began to preach "repent ye," the people sat up, listened, and repented in sackcloth and ashes. What was the sign Jonah bore? He bore no proof of authenticity but the power of the message he proclaimed.

People still want signs from God to prove God is at work. I'm not one to try to put God to the test. If you want to do that, it's your business. But, friend, I'm not going to have any part of it. I'm never going to say, "God, if you'll do this, I'll do this, and you show me this is what you want me to do, and I'll do it." I want God's revelation and I want to know God's will, but I'm not going to put any fleece out and say, "Lord, You wet it tonight and dry it off miraculously tomorrow and I'll know." None of that for me. Sign-seekers were labeled by our Lord to be wicked and adulterous.

There are people today who openly assert that speaking in an unknown tongue is a sign from heaven. Many of these same people have a penchant for Paul, but they are guilty of isolating the teachings of Paul.

In 1 Corinthians 12:31 one can see what Paul has to say. He is talking about the problems connected with spiritual gifts, and in chapters 12 and 14 he's talking about the unknown tongue and related matters. After discussing these spiritual gifts through chapter 12 he reaches the end of that chapter writing, "But covet earnestly the best gifts: and yet shew I unto you a more excellent way." Now what is the more excellent way? It's the thirteenth chapter, the chapter on love. Paul is convinced that a whole lot better than the gift of tongues is the gift of love, and that's what every Christian ought to seek. You ought to seek to love like Jesus loved. That's the best gift. Don't settle for anything less, for if you have the finest, highest, and best gift, then love never faileth. Love will find a way. There will be no problem you'll face but that there will be an answer to it. Paul states openly and positively that the more excellent way is the way of love. That ought to be clear. Paul said he had spoken in tongues, but the best way is the way of love. That's the teaching of Paul and the summation of the matter. Don't be sidetracked by anything leading up to the ultimate. The ultimate is the way of love. That is the highest and the best gift. Paul even suggested that though he spoke with the tongues of men and angels and did not have love, what was he? Nothing. Just like pounding on a cymbal and clanging brass; just like an empty, hollow, meaningless noise.

So tongues-speaking is not the ultimate. It's in a lesser category. Paul put it way down the line. The best gift, the highest aspiration in the heart of a Christian ought to be to love like Jesus loved. The sign we display to the world ought to be the same sign New Testament Christians displayed. That sign is embodied in the incredulous remark, "Behold how they love one another." That's the way the world knows that we know Jesus, when they see us loving each other. Not cutting, loving. Not criticizing, loving. Not maligning, loving. Not exhibiting hard-heartedness, but exhibiting love. Not an unwillingness to forgive, but love! When we don't have it, the world puts a question mark over our lives and our witness, and rightly so! The highest and best gift is love.

Another aspect of the confusion that exists in our day focuses on human experience versus the teachings of the Bible. Don't ever elevate the experience you might claim above the revelation of God in his Word. If what you have experienced is not validated by the teachings of the Word of God, then your experience is suspect.

Tongues-speaking is not confined to those who claim to be Christians. Tongues-speaking is also indulged in by Muslims, Buddhists, Confucianists, and young people coming out of the drug culture, all claiming the same gift. It's for that reason alone that we can't say tongues-speaking validates the Christian experience. It cannot be a validation, because there are those who are not Christians who also claim that experience. Human experience cannot be elevated above the Word of God. Feelings are not reliable guidelines in Christian living.

I could name right now, almost from memory, two dozen people I know in our city who have said to me, "Preacher, when I get the feeling, or when I feel like it, I'm going to come and make a profession of faith." They're waiting on a feeling. There's not a verse of Scripture to be found in Old or New Testament that says that you become a Christian, that you're saved, that you receive the new birth, by a feeling. You receive God's gift of salvation when you meet his terms. The feeling comes later.

You don't feel like a married man until you get married. You don't feel like a Christian feels until you become a Christian. You don't get the feeling first. You follow God's outline first, his clear guidelines, and when you do the feeling comes and it's authenticated by the teachings of the Word of God. The Bible is the divine yardstick. Lay the Bible down alongside every human experience. Anything you and I have experienced that cannot be substantiated in the teachings of the Book is not valid.

My daddy use to say the test of whether or not the Holy Spirit has you is not how high you jump when he hits you, it's how straight you walk when you hit the ground. I believe that's true. The test of whether or not the Holy Spirit possesses you is not the moment of ecstasy you might have at a given time. The test of whether or not the Holy Spirit has you is how straight you walk when you hit the ground. Do you love like Jesus loved? Do you possess the fruits of the Spirit found in Galatians 5? That probably is the valid yardstick which needs to be laid down alongside human experience.

Look at another reference. In 1 John 4:1–2 we are reminded to do exactly what we are doing. "Beloved, believe not every spirit, but try the spirits whether they are of God: because many false prophets are gone out into the world. Hereby know ye the Spirit of God: Every spirit that confesseth that Jesus Christ is come in the flesh is of God." Try the spirits. That means there are false spirits. That means a person can say something with his lips and not be able to back it up with his life.

Confused people, in our day, present to the world a most unfortunate dichotomy between receiving Jesus Christ and receiving the Holy Spirit. I'm going to tell you why I'm saying that. They leave the impression with the whole world that the Holy Spirit gives a greater and richer blessing than one receives through taking Christ as Savior. They are saying, in their literature and with their lips, that the greatest experience of their lives has been the experience with the Holy Spirit and speaking in tongues.

This implies that Jesus Christ is not God's complete and final gift for redemption. I'm saying when you received Jesus Christ, you received all God has to offer! I'm saying that Jesus Christ is the power of God, and the wisdom of God, and I'm going to validate that with 1 Corinthians 1:23–24. Turn to that if you will. "But we preach Christ crucified, unto the Jews a stumbling block, and unto the Greeks foolishness. But unto them which are called, both Jews and Greeks, Christ the power of God, and the wisdom of God." Now when you received Jesus Christ, what did you receive? You received the power of God, which is the power of the Holy Spirit, and you received the wisdom of God. The power of God, of the Holy Spirit, and the wisdom of God are all wrapped up in what you received in Jesus Christ.

Now look at verse 30 in this same chapter. "But of him [that is, of God] are ye in Christ Jesus, who of God is made unto us wisdom, and righteousness, and sanctification, and redemption." It's all wrapped up in our receiving Jesus Christ as Savior. When you receive Jesus Christ, you receive all wisdom, all righteousness, all sanctification, and all redemption. It is, therefore, a kind of sign-seeking plus a denial of the teachings of the Word of God to look for anything outside of and beyond Jesus Christ. I can't accept it. The Bible says that in Jesus Christ we have all God has to offer. To receive him is to receive all God has.

Now if you don't believe that, turn to Colossians 2:9–10. In that chapter we find exactly what I'm saying substantiated. This is the Word of God, not my opinion. This is not some belief I have conjured up, this is God speaking to our hearts. "For in him . . ." Now who is "him?" Look at the last word of verse 8 and you'll find out: Christ. "For in [Christ] dwelleth all of the fulness of the Godhead bodily. And ye are complete in him." Now, brother, I didn't say it, I read it and if you don't believe it, that's your business. I believe it. God said it, I believe and that settles it in my mind.

This verse goes on to say, "which is the head of all principality and power." When you receive Jesus Christ, you receive all of the fullness of the Godhead bodily. Now you, if you've received Jesus Christ, on the basis of your repentance and through faith, are complete in him. You don't need anything added to receiving Jesus Christ. You've received all that God has to offer.

When someone poses this dichotomy and says you receive Christ over here and receive the baptism of the Holy Spirit over there, they simply are not consistent with the teachings of the Word of God, which is tantamount to a rejection of the Word of God. Anything that adds to or subtracts from the Word of God is a form of blasphemy, and confusion.

Now look for a moment at a—

Comparison.

The comparison to which I refer is between Jesus and John the Baptist. The verse we took from Matthew's Gospel was the word of John. The verse we took from Acts was the word of Jesus. John is truly a prophet sent from God. He is the only man about whom our blessed Lord said, "Of all the men born of woman there has not arisen a greater than John the Baptist." When you get an accolade like that you've reached the pinnacle. Jesus said the finest thing about John the Baptist he could say. He said of all the men born of woman there has not arisen a greater than John the Baptist, and Jesus knew about Moses, Abraham, Isaac, Jacob, and all the Old Testament patriarchs. There is not a one greater than John the Baptist.

John spoke of carrying the sandals of Jesus. This was a task that usually fell to the humblest slave in a household. The slave that had the least talent and who couldn't do anything else walked around and carried the master's sandals. Whenever the master went outside, he was there to give him his sandals. John said, "When you compare me with Jesus, I'm just like that slave who can't do anything. The dumb one. The dumb-dumb who can't do anything but carry sandals; I'm like that slave in comparison with

Jesus, who's the master of the household." John said there is no comparison.

Then came the natural comparison between the baptism of John and the baptism of Jesus. John said, "I indeed baptize you with water unto [the King James says] repentance." Now that little Greek particle translated "unto" is the Greek particle *eis*. It's translated in a variety of ways in the New Testament, the translation depending upon the construction in which it's used. In this construction that particle can be translated, and should be translated "on the basis of." John said, "I baptize you with water" (on the basis of) "your repentance." Not *unto*, not *for* repentance. In other words, "I don't baptize you in order that you might repent. I baptize you *because* you have repented, on the basis of your repentance I baptize you." And then he said: "The one coming after me is mightier than I. I'm not even worthy to carry his shoes, and he's going to baptize you with the Holy Ghost and with fire."

Now, frankly, this Scripture doesn't have any significance for people who sprinkle instead of immerse. It doesn't have any meaning, for if you were to substitute sprinkling for immersion here, which is not allowable exegetically, you would completely rob this of its force. John's baptism was complete submersion in water. It was inundation, immersion.

Christ's baptism, in the Holy Ghost, is going to be overwhelming and completely possessing of the soul. John, a divinely commissioned prophet, baptized symbolically in water. Jesus Christ, the Son of God, crowned his redemptive work on the day of Pentecost and in the life of every believer in the baptism of the Holy Spirit.

Now in my judgment this baptism cannot refer to water baptism. When you're baptized in the Holy Spirit, this has no reference to water baptism. This is rather the baptism referred to in Ephesians 4:5. "One Lord, one faith, one baptism." Now that could not be a reference to water baptism, because of the context in which that verse appears. This is the baptism by which we become members of the body of Christ and of the family of God.

Now if all of this had reference to water baptism, what would that do to John 4:2? Look at this verse. "Though Jesus himself baptized not." I'm saying if water baptism was essential to salvation, Jesus would have been busy baptizing everybody he could. Jesus said, "No man cometh unto the Father but by me," and if baptism, water baptism, were essential to salvation, Jesus would have been busy baptizing.

So these references undoubtedly refer to the baptism of the Holy Spirit, "One Lord, one faith, one baptism," whereby we become members of the body of Christ. We're submerged by the Holy Spirit, who applies the blood of Jesus Christ in the life of a sinner, and that experience is completely overwhelming and possessing. It doesn't imply sinlessness, it implies possession. We, by that submersion in the power of the Holy Spirit, become members of the body of Christ, we are born into God's family, we become his and he becomes ours in a new and vital relationship.

Now on this same thought turn to 1 Corinthians 1:14. In that passage the apostle Paul, following the same pattern of Jesus Christ said, "I thank God that I baptized none of you, but Crispus and Gaius." Now if water baptism were essential to salvation, do you think the apostle Paul would have thanked God that he hadn't had the opportunity to baptize but two people? I think not. I think the absurdity of that view is easily seen.

On the basis of these verses, one Lord, one faith, one baptism undoubtedly refers to the baptism of the Holy Spirit which we receive in the moment we receive Jesus Christ, who is the fullness of all the Godhead bodily.

Let's draw some definite—

Conclusions.

Look, if you will, in the sixteenth chapter of the Gospel of John, verses 13 and 14. This is a flat assertion of a definite truth. "Howbeit when he, the Spirit of truth is come, he will guide you into all truth: for he shall not speak of himself; but whatsoever he shall hear, that shall he speak: and he will shew you things to come. He shall glorify me: [Jesus] for he shall receive of mine, and shall shew it unto you." It is the purpose of God's Holy Spirit to glorify Jesus Christ. The Holy Spirit does not speak of himself, neither does one who is filled with the Holy Spirit. Are you hearing me? I'm saying that those who go around magnifying and exalting the Holy Spirit do not possess him, for those who possess the Holy Spirit go about magnifying and exalting Jesus. The work of the Holy Spirit is to make men Christ-conscious, not Holy Spirit-conscious.

The apostle Paul in 1 Corinthians 14:19 said something we need to heed. Look at it. "Yet in the church I had rather speak five words with my understanding, that by my voice I might teach others also, than ten thousand words in an unknown tongue." I am not a mathematician, but it seems to me that the ratio is two thousand to one. If that be true, it's a whole lot better to say "Jesus" one time than to say two thousand "pig-latins." I don't care what the jabbers are or who interprets them, one time to say Jesus where people can understand you is a whole lot better than to talk at length in a way no one understands.

On the day of Pentecost Simon Peter was the leader of the Pentecostal movement. He was filled with the power of the Holy Spirit, and when he was, he didn't go out before men to tell them about an experience. Are you reading me? He didn't go out and tell them what had happened to him. He didn't talk about the fact that they could speak in a language they had never studied where men who spoke that language could understand the gospel. He didn't talk about that. He talked about Jesus Christ and him crucified.

Read in Acts 2:22 what Peter said. "Ye men of Israel, hear these words: I just had the baptism of the Holy Spirit and can speak in an unknown. . . ." Is that what he said? "Jesus of Nazareth, a man approved of God among you by miracles and wonders and signs, which God did by him in the midst of you, as ye yourselves also know." What did he say? He went on to preach Jesus alive, risen from the dead, and ready in that moment, to save all who would come to him in faith and in trust.

The baptism of the Holy Spirit is a once and for all gift from God at the moment of conversion, and when one has received that experience, the baptism of the Holy Spirit, this new birth, he starts talking about Jesus. He doesn't talk about the Holy Spirit, he doesn't try to magnify anybody or anything except the living Christ who comes into the hearts of men in power and makes them new creatures.

To be filled with the Spirit involves the power for our task. This filling, which comes in moments of submission throughout life, enables prophets and apostles and believers to speak the Word of God with boldness.

Check out these references to the filling of the Holy Spirit: Acts 4:8; Acts 4:31; Acts 9:17; Acts 13:9; Ephesians 5:18. These and other Scriptures reveal that when one is filled with the Spirit of God he is bold in his witness for the Lord Jesus Christ.

John said of Jesus, "He shall baptize you in the Holy Ghost and with fire." Fire is used in several ways in the Bible. One usage of it describes hell, eternal punishment, and the judgment of God. The hell of fire burns up the chaff, consumes the tares, and punishes the wicked and wickedness eternally.

The other usage of the word "fire" in the New Testament alludes to the refiner's fire. It's the fire that becomes the agent to separate dross and make the metal pure. You were baptized in the Holy Spirit, receiving the fullness of God's offer and God's redemption in the moment you trusted Jesus. Wouldn't you admit that there is a need for the refiner's fire, separating the dross in your life, and leaving your life pure and unsullied so Christ is reflected in you? I am sure there are many persons who would confess the need for that experience. I am here to tell you that Jesus Christ is ready to give you what you need in order to be an effective witness for him to honor and magnify his name.

The uppermost question has to do with your relationship with

Christ. Have you really trusted him as your Savior? Was the experience real? If it was, God gave you all he had in that moment. He gave you wisdom, power, righteousness, and sanctification. He gave you everything good you could possibly want and ever use. If you've had this experience of conversion, God's Spirit is within you. He's ready to fill you and empower you for service. If you've never trusted Christ, now is the time to make that decision.

10. The Spirit's Pain
EPHESIANS 4:30–32

The Ephesian epistle probably was a circular letter addressed to more than one church. The membership of the churches to which Paul wrote included Jews and Gentiles, between whom the wall of separation had been removed. They had some of the same problems in that day we have in our day. Theirs was a problem of prejudice and animosity between the races. The only difference is that in Paul's and Jesus' day it was animosity between Jew and Gentile whereas in our day it's between whites and blacks, or people whose skin happens to be a different color from our own. The apostle Paul was addressing himself to precisely this problem in his Ephesian epistle.

He's saying that the faith we have in Jesus Christ is a unified faith. It's a faith marked by oneness. It's characterized, as he points out, by one Lord, the Lord Jesus, one faith, that's faith in him and salvation by grace through that faith, and one baptism.

Now this is not water baptism. This is the baptism of the Holy Spirit. It's the baptism whereby we are sealed. This baptism is equivalent to, synonymous with, the new birth. It's the experience we have when we are converted, when we ask Jesus Christ to come into our hearts, for when he does the Holy Spirit comes in also.

When we receive Jesus, we receive all God has to offer. We don't receive Jesus at one time and receive the Holy Spirit later. We receive everything God offers when we trust Christ and invite him to come into our hearts.

The truth of the fullness of salvation is revealed in the words of Colossians 2:9–10. Look at the last word of verse 8. In the King

James translation that word is "Christ." Taking up in verse 9, we read, "For in him [Who is that? Christ! The last word of verse 8, Christ] dwelleth all the fulness of the Godhead bodily." In other words, everything God the Father is, Jesus was. "In him [Jesus] dwelt all the fulness of the Godhead bodily."

Now look at verse 10: "And ye are complete in him." That means when you received Jesus Christ, you received all God offers. You may not have appropriated it all, you may not have understood it, you may not have come to a realization of all you had at your disposal, but God gave it to you nevertheless. It's all yours in Jesus Christ.

So this baptism, which is the baptism of the Holy Spirit coming at the moment that we, through faith, receive one Lord, even Jesus, means that the inner man is completely submerged in the power of God's Spirit. The baptism of the Holy Spirit means that our personalities are enveloped in his power. We're wrapped up in the power of Almighty God.

This experience is attested to by water baptism. Water baptism is an external symbol of an internal experience. Water baptism, coming after conversion, says to the world, "I have been as totally submerged in the power of God's Spirit in the inner man as I am being totally submerged in this water as a symbol of that experience." One Lord, one faith, one baptism.

A preacher friend told of an experience that was his which is rather common to humans. He went into a department store to make a purchase and, to his dismay, found it was the day of a bargain sale. The store was crowded to capacity, people were clogging all the aisles. He immediately found the article he was seeking, but then he went through the tedious, frustrating experience of trying to get a clerk to wait on him. He looked in every direction and his anxiety mounted. Finally, out of nowhere a clerk appeared and in a sweet voice asked, "May I help you?" Of course she could and she did, while all his erstwhile frustration and anxiety vanished.

That's precisely the question God's Holy Spirit is asking every Christian. He came into your heart in the moment of conversion and every minute of the day he's asking, "May I help you?"

Recall the experience of the Israelites in their pilgrimage between Egypt, the land of bondage, and the Promised Land. Forty years they wandered in that sojourn, but all the time God wanted them to have the Promised Land. He wanted them to have delights they had never imagined. He wanted that inheritance to be theirs and was ready to give it to them, but they wouldn't take it. Forty years they wandered around murmuring and discontented. God wanted them to have the best, but they weren't willing to accept it. That's so powerfully descriptive of our lives, for God wants you and me to have much more than we have ever received from him.

There are two kinds of electric current. These two kinds are AC and DC, alternating current and direct current. Alternating current is on a cycle. Sixty cycles of current per second and sixty cycles of no current per second alternating off and on, constantly alternating. DC, or direct current, such as is derived from a battery or a storage cell, does not alternate. It comes constantly.

Broadly speaking, we find here the approach most of us take to the Holy Spirit, either AC or DC. We either take from him his power and gifts, his blessings, in an alternating fashion or we try to live our lives in direct contact with him and in so doing experience the overcoming, victorious life. God wants to provide DC, direct current, direct contact in your life and mine. The Holy Spirit is here now, in our hearts, ready to provide for us.

In our text Paul began with a clear—

Negation.

The negation is "grieve not the Holy Spirit." In other words don't do it. Don't grieve God's Spirit. Do you realize that our actions out of the will of God cause pain to the Father God and his Spirit? At the moment of conversion, the Holy Spirit took up residence in your life. He has available all of the resources of heaven's storehouse, yet when the Holy Spirit came in he did not override your free moral choice. He did not put you in a moral straightjacket where you'd have to do what he said do. He came in, he abides in you and me, but he leaves us with the power to choose. You can either choose right or wrong. We either exercise our moral choice in righteousness or unrighteousness, for as Jesus once said, "According to your faith be it unto you." He who has redeemed us and resides within us rejoices in our victories over sin, but is deeply grieved and pained over our defeat and failures.

We're born into the family of God at the moment of conversion, but you know, we're not born full grown. You were born into the family of your parents, but you weren't born full grown. You came in about eight, six, or maybe ten pounds of human flesh, and since that day you've grown. You would be a sad specimen if you had remained a baby, physically speaking. You would have been a rarity, an oddity, an object of pity if you had failed to grow physically from the moment of your birth. How many of us are there as Christians who have never grown in the faith?

You see, the proof of salvation is revealed externally in our new manner of life. One shows his transference from darkness to light, from the devil's dominion to the kingdom of God through his flesh, his life-style, his manner of living. He reveals to the world that the works of the flesh fall away, and there is a new spirituality in evidence. We reveal the fruits of the Spirit, proving beyond doubt that something has taken place on the inside. Every failure at that point grieves the Spirit of God.

Go back to the very first words in Ephesians 4:1. "I, therefore, the prisoner of the Lord, beseech you that ye walk worthy." That's what he's talking about in verses 30 through 32. He's referring to a worthy walk which does not grieve the Holy Spirit. The unworthy walk causes pain in the heart of God.

The Holy Spirit is grieved when we belittle the Word of God. We show our love for God, for his Son and for the Holy Spirit through our reverence and love for the Bible. The Bible is the only authoritative, written source of information we have regarding God the Father, his Son, the Holy Spirit, and our admonitions to walk in the faith. Ignorance of the Bible, indifference toward a study of the Bible, neglect of the teachings of the Bible, and an unconcern for the proclamation of the gospel causes deep grief to the Holy Spirit.

I'm saying, in case you're not yet with me, that when you're not concerned for Bible knowledge you're causing the Holy Spirit grief. When you don't avail yourself of the opportunity to study the Book and learn more of the teachings of Jesus, you're remaining spiritually atrophied, a spiritual pygmy, a dwarf when you ought to be a giant for God in the life you live.

In addition to this negation "grieve not the Spirit" Paul adds a—

Notation.

The notation is "whereby we are sealed." The seal of the Holy Spirit is a guarantee. It's the seal or guarantee that your redemption has been completed. You never have to do anything other than receive Jesus Christ in order for salvation to be complete. The transaction is finished. That is only the beginning of your Christian life, but the transaction is finished in Jesus Christ. "In him dwelleth all the fulness of the Godhead bodily. And ye are complete in him " (Col. 2:9–10).

God doesn't perform second works of grace to complete salvation. He doesn't add some so-called second blessing out in the future. When you receive Jesus Christ, you receive everything God has to offer, yet at that moment you are a baby and you're to begin the Christian walk and grow in your likeness of Jesus.

You're sealed by the Holy Spirit and this is God's guarantee of eternal security. This is your possession as an individual. It is God's promise never to let you be lost. You have that guarantee. That guarantee is the seal of the Holy Spirit.

I know literally thousands of people who claim to be saved, but who have no joy in their salvation. Joy is missing because they are afraid they are going to lose what they've got. It you go through life fearful that you're going to lose salvation, that you're going to be lost at some future time, you're not ever going to serve Christ as fully as you could. It's only when you have the assurance of the constancy of God's love and grace and redemption that you can serve God with freedom and abandon. That's why God gives the seal of the Holy Spirit. "Whereby we are sealed."

To be sealed represents an ancient practice by which a transaction was consummated. When the king issued an official proclamation, his officers would take a candle and drop hot wax on the bottom of that document. The king's seal, which ordinarily was a signet ring, was turned and placed in that hot wax. Anyone who saw that seal knew the king himself had put his imprimatur upon it and that his office guaranteed the validity of it.

That's what God does in the Holy Spirit. When the Holy Spirit came into our hearts at the moment of conversion, we were sealed by him. This is God's guarantee that we can never, never, never be lost. This represents finality. It means the matter is closed. The Holy Spirit seals us in a relationship with the Father God and Jesus Christ that will never be severed.

Someone comes along to say, "You know, if you can be saved like that you can go out and live any way you want to." Is that right? Where did you get that idea? You certainly didn't get it from the pages of God's Word, for if you'll look in the eighth chapter of Romans, you'll find a very interesting truth in verse 14. Does a person who is saved go out and live like the devil and say, "Well, so what, I'm already saved so it doesn't matter how I live." No! Verse 14 says: "As many as are led by the Spirit of God, they are the sons of God." Does the child of God go out in a wild orgy of sin, presuming on eternal security? No, for the Holy Spirit does not lead a child of God in that way and you are only a child of God if you are led by the Spirit of God within you. If you're God's child, God's Spirit leads you in the ways of righteousness revealing to the world that your commitment is real, and proving God lives within you.

In 2 Corinthians 1:21–22 we learn that the Spirit of God has sealed us and the Holy Spirit is the earnest of God's redemption. Most of us here have purchased articles on the lay-away plan or on an installment payment plan. On a lay-away plan you pick out an article you wish to purchase and give the store an amount of money which requires the store to hold that article until you come to claim it.

This is comparable to the earnest of God's Spirit. He is the down payment. At the moment of salvation we have the earnest of the Spirit, God's down payment, guaranteeing he will finish the transaction, that there's more to come, that this is not all, but that God is coming to claim us on the glorious day of the return of Jesus Christ. Then the earnest of the Spirit will be "bought up," we'll be his eternally in an unbroken relationship, face to face with Christ our Savior. The down payment has already been made, and every true believer knows that the down payment has been made in his behalf because of the earnest of the Holy Spirit. The final transaction is yet to come, but we have the joy of salvation and the assurance of eternal security by the seal and earnest of the Holy Spirit.

In the third place Paul gives us in these verses a—

Norm.

A norm is a standard, it's the normal way of life for the Christian. Our normal way of life is this: "Put away therefore all bitterness, wrath, anger, clamor, slander, and all malice, and be ye kind . . ."

Don't you think that is one of the biggest hangups most of us have? In our Christian walk we discover we're just not kind. In the Greek there's an interesting comparison between the word *kind* and the word *Christ*. The word kind is *chrestos*, c-h-r-e-s-t-o-s, transliterated in English. C-h-r-e-s-t-o-s, *chrestos*. The word Christ in Greek is *Christos*, C-h-r-i-s-t-o-s. *Chrestos—Christos*. The only difference between "kind" and "Christ" is one letter. I think that's significant, for if we are followers of Christ we are required to be kind one to another, tenderhearted.

Do you know the difference between being tenderhearted and hardhearted? Being tenderhearted means you're willing to admit that you are wrong. It involves being willing to apologize. It implies being willing to accept blame, whereas hardheartedness involves trying to point the accusing finger at someone else.

I don't know a home in America that's in trouble but that could get back on a solid rock if kindness prevailed. "Be ye kind one to another." It ought to start in the home and touch all of life's relationships. "Tenderhearted, forgiving one another as God in Christ forgave you."

I know people who are spending their lives trying to "get even." I know people just waiting for the right moment when they can really "show" somebody. I know those who are harboring hatred and fueling the fires of anger by waiting for the right moment to really get somebody told. "The very next time this or this happens, I'm going to really tell him or her off." "Grieve not the Holy Spirit." That's the way you grieve him, you see. You grieve him with bitterness and wrath and anger and clamor and slander and malice. You cause him to rejoice when you are like Christ, kind one to another.

About all a person ever proves who has bitterness and anger and unforgiveness is that the Spirit of God is not in him. If he is a Christian, to say the very least he's operating on alternating current and not direct current.

The fruits of the Spirit are in total contrast to the works of the flesh. The works of the flesh are those we put off to reveal the new man in Christ Jesus.

Maybe someone asks now, "How can I get the Holy Spirit?" The answer is in Luke 11:13. There Jesus said so plainly: "If ye then being evil, know how to give good gifts to your children: how much more shall your heavenly Father give the Holy Spirit to them that ask him." If you know how to do good things for your kids at Christmas, on their birthdays, and at other times, if you've got that much kindness in your heart, how much more will God do for those who ask the Holy Spirit!

God is tapping on your shoulder even now asking, "May I help you?" He's ready right now to do for you what you can never do for yourself. When you fail to surrender, when you're hardhearted, you put the Holy Spirit on AC and cause him grief and pain. God wants you to have the best he offers, but he can only give on the basis of your surrender. When you become tenderhearted, admitting your weakness and failures, admitting when you've been wrong and have sinned against him and grieved him, then come and receive direct current straight from the storehouse of heaven.

11. The Spirit's Partnership
GALATIANS 5:16

Walking in the Spirit ought to be the hourly experience of every child of God. The Greek verb here, which is in the imperative, actually means "walking around." The prefix on this verb is the prefix *peri* which means around. *Peripateo* is the Greek verb, to walk around. Paul says its imperative for you to walk around in the Spirit.

Now I want to tell you something. This is not an experience that comes to you after a certain number of years of Christian growth. This is the way of Christian growth. You don't grow as a Christian unless or until you walk around in the Spirit.

We've dealt with a number of the facets of the ministry of the Holy Spirit. We have considered the personality of the Holy Spirit, the power, the presence, the pervasion, the possession, the pursuit, the purpose, and the pain. We've talked about the Spirit perverted and now we're discussing partnership with the Holy Spirit. We also have a chapter on "Test the Tongues," all having to do with the work and ministry of God's Holy Spirit. Now we are talking about the Spirit's partnership and I maintain that this is a—

Happy

—holy, and helpful walk.

I'm grateful for happy music. That's the way it ought to be. The missing ingredient in the life of many believers is happiness or joy. A morose, unhappy Christian is a contradiction of terms. Forgiveness and eternal salvation bring eternal joy.

There are two Scripture passages basic at this point. One of these is 1 Corinthians 6:19: "Know ye not that your body is the temple of the Holy Spirit which is in you, which ye have of God?" Body. The word body has to do with this physical entity. That means the Holy Spirit came into this body, not just your soul, your body, at the moment you received Jesus Christ as your Savior. He's in you! He's the one who provides joy and assurance. If you've been cleansed and converted, the Spirit of God is in you.

There's a second verse basic to our understanding here. This is in the eighth chapter of Romans, verse 16: "The Spirit [himself] beareth witness with our spirit, that we are the children of God." I'm contending that when the Spirit of God lives in this mortal body, in our souls and our bodies, the victory and assurance he gives makes every other matter inconsequential by comparison. There is an overriding joy in Christ. That's why the apostle Paul urged us to give thanks in all things, or rejoice in all things.

Now there are some things that would not seem to be sources of joy, but if we'll rejoice in the midst of them and accept them as opportunities to glorify God and give a strong witness for him, the Lord will give us joy and he'll make our witness more effective.

If you can have the Holy Spirit in you and not know it, you can lose him and never miss him. I'm asking you, right now, do you have the Holy Spirit within you? How do you know? Do you know because of the way you feel? Maybe, but there's a far greater reason. You have the Holy Spirit within you, if you're saved, because God has promised him. That transcends your feelings. That eliminates your ups and downs, whether or not you feel like it, whether you're happy or sad. God has said it; that settles it!

God's Word teaches in the moment of your conversion you receive everything he has to offer, including the Holy Spirit. Now if he's within you, everything else can pale into insignificance, because the important thing is you have victory in Jesus Christ.

Walking around in the Spirit is a happy walk because the Holy Spirit not only assures of salvation, but he satisfies forever. Are you satisfied as a Christian or do you keep feeling something is missing?

Let me remind you of an experience Jesus had with a Samaritan woman. Recently showing some pictures we took in Israel, I showed a picture of Jacob's well. Our party visited there in the summer of 1972. Many of us drank water from Jacob's well. When Jesus dealt with this Samaritan woman in the present-day city of Nablus, he said, "You know, if you drink from the water of this well it's not really going to slake your thirst." This is in the fourth chapter of John, verses 13 and 14. He said, "If you drink this water you'll get thirsty again."

But he added, "If you drink the water I shall give you, you will never thirst." I think that's important. The Holy Spirit satisfies forever. You find church members who are always looking for something new, something a little bizarre and offbeat, some new spiritual thrill, some spiritual "high" that they have never experienced. I say they are missing something, for when we drink the water that Jesus gives, we'll never thirst again. That means he satisfies us spiritually with the positive assurance of salvation, with his presence, and with the promise of power available to us in the hour of need that shall always be adequate.

I don't need ever have any doubt about God's goodness, about his ability to help me in a time of need. He's settled that matter once and for all, and I'm satisfied in my mind that my God is able.

Drink from the fountain of wealth and it creates a greater thirst. Drink from the fountain of worldly acclaim and your thirst for fame grows. Drink from the fountain of worldly pleasure or sexual impurity or an illicit relationship, or drink from the fountain of human knowledge, and you'll thirst again and again and again. But our blessed Lord gave the Samaritan woman the assurance that he gives you and me: "The water that I shall give him shall in him be a well of water springing up into everlasting life." There's always a sufficiency to slake the thirst of the one who is in Christ.

I'm maintaining that the Spirit's partnership is a happy walk. You walk around in the Spirit, and you won't walk with a long face. The world won't have to question whether or not you've been saved. They'll see in you the radiance of your relationship. It's a happy walk.

Walking around in the Spirit is a—

Holy

—walk. This is the kind of holiness based on faith and not on works.

Most of you recall the verse that was so meaningful to Martin Luther, the former Roman Catholic priest, one of those who caused the Protestant Reformation. Hebrews 10:38 is the verse, "The just shall live by faith." That eliminates works, doesn't it? The just, or that is those who are justified, shall live by faith. That's where it is. That's where the action is. It's not in how many times we have done this, or how much we have given, or how many hours we have spent in this or that spiritual pursuit. The just shall live by faith!

Paul assured us in 2 Corinthians 5:7, "For we walk by faith, not by sight." The Christian, then, who is walking around in the Spirit, takes one step at a time and he takes that step by faith. He's not walking by what he can see, he's not walking by what he feels, but he's walking with an utter dependence upon the incarnate Word, revealed in the written Word by the Holy Spirit of God.

The caption on our bulletin board recently said: "Faith is walking to the edge of all the light you have, and then taking one more step." You never take the step of faith as long as you can see it, as long as you know where your foot will be planted. The step of faith comes when you move into the area of the unknown. That's the only kind of faith the world really notices.

When the world says that what we do as Christians is being done in human strength or as a result of promotional ability or of an extensive advertizing campaign or as a result of whipping up our faded, jaded nerves, the world yawns and says, "Well, they're just like everybody else." But when lost people see Christians walking by faith, going to the edge of all of the light that we have and then taking one more step, the world says: "They've got something. I don't know what they've got, but they've got something." "The just shall live by faith."

The walk of faith is a holy walk, but to our faith must be added obedience. You really don't have Christian faith unless you are obedient. In John 14:21 Jesus said: "He that hath my commandments, and keepeth them, he it is that loveth me." That's the reason for my skepticism over some aspects of the Jesus Movement on the part of certain young people. When they mouth these pious platitudes and say how much they love Jesus and live in open disobedience to Jesus, I don't believe them! Jesus said: "He that hath my commandments and keepeth them, he it is that loveth me."

He said it another way in another place. "If you love me, keep my commandments." Now I want to give you a Leavell translation of that: "If you love me, mind me! If you love me, do what I said do." If you don't do what he said do, it's pretty obvious you don't love him. The only way you or I can reveal Christ is to obey Christ. When we obey him, the unsaved can see him in us. We're not living our lives, we're living his life. We live his life when we live in obedience to his commands.

I've never known a child of God walking around in the Spirit who was unsure of his salvation. Jesus admonished certain of his disciples, "Watch and pray that ye enter not into temptation. The Spirit indeed is willing but the flesh is weak." That's another reason walking around in the Spirit is a holy walk, for it's marked by watchfulness and prayer. A Christian isn't stupid. A Christian is watchful and prayerful. A Christian is alert. A Christian understands what's going on around him. A Christian knows who he is and where he is going.

One of the things Bob Harrington said stuck in my mind. He recounted a conversation he had with a hippy type down in the French Quarter in New Orleans. After they had talked for thirty minutes or so, this hippy said to him, "I feel sorry for you, believing all of these antiquated, passé ideas about Christianity. I feel sorry for you." Bob said, "Don't feel sorry for me." He asked, "Why?" Bob answered, "Because I know some things you don't know. I know who I am and I know where I'm going!" A Christian isn't stupid. A Christian knows who he is and where's he's going.

He understands he's living in enemy territory. There's never a time when we can look upon this world as our home. There's never a time we can look forward to but that we'll be beset by the presence of the enemy. The devil is the prince of the powers of this world and this is his domain. Christians know that. If you're walking around in the Spirit, you know that the walk is not going to be peaceful. You know that there will never be a moment when you'll be exempt from temptation and the lure of sin. Satan still hates God. He still uses every means at his disposal to combat holiness. When you walk around in the Spirit you know that.

You see, in the Christian warfare there's no truce. You're not afforded any moments when you can catch your breath or replenish your resources. The Christian is in constant, unceasing, unrelenting warfare and it's real. It's just as real for us as it was for Jesus our Lord.

So the Christian walk, walking around in the Spirit, is a holy walk because we obey Jesus instead of obeying the devil. Let me add the third word. The Christian walk, walking in the Spirit, is a—

Helpful

—walk. In 1 John 1:7 we read: "If we walk in the light, as he [Jesus] is in the light, we have fellowship one with another, and the blood of Jesus Christ his Son cleanseth us from all sin." There is no denying that when we walk in the Spirit we walk in fellowship, and if you're out of fellowship you're not walking in the Spirit. I didn't say it, I read it, and if you don't believe it, you're not renouncing what I say, you're renouncing the Book. It's in the Book. If you're out of fellowship with other human beings, you're not walking around in the Spirit, because if we walk in the light as he is in the light we have fellowship one with another. We love each other. Fellowship implies helpfulness.

Now, I'm going to take the middlebuster and plow up some corn right here. It's going to get the roots exposed and there may be some scorching. If you're walking in the Spirit, you're not primarily concerned about your own convenience! It won't make much difference to you how you've always done it. It will make a lot of difference to you how you can do it best.

I'm saying this to those of you who do things only because that's the way you've always done them. I'm saying you might take another look at things. If changing your sequence might be helpful in reaching lost people for Jesus and reaching some babes in Christ with nurture and admonition to the faith, then what do you think you ought to do? Do you want to be helpful or hurtful? Do you want to keep on doing something because of your own convenience or do you want to honor Christ by reaching people for him? I'm saying if you walk around in the Spirit, that's going to be a helpful walk! You're going to help other people by doing it.

I want to say something else about fellowship. Fellowship is always open. It's never closed, it's never secret. You do not have the prerogative of choosing who can be included. You don't have the choice, if you're a Christian walking around in the Spirit, of saying, "I'm not going to have fellowship with him or with them." You can't say, "His skin is a different color from mine and I don't want to have fellowship with him!" If you're walking around in the Spirit, you don't have that option. The only option you have is to fellowship with whomsoever the Spirit fellowships, and if this is Christ's church the only option that's ours is to accept all whom Christ accepts!

If ours isn't Christ's church and really belongs to a few of us, then we make up our minds about who can come and who can't. We ought to take the name Christ out of anything and everything we do if this is not his church, for we're not following him at all when we close our fellowship or make it secret. To shut someone out or to cut someone off from human fellowship in Christ reveals that we're not walking after the Spirit, we're walking after the flesh.

Christian fellowship does not work under cover or behind people's backs. Christian fellowship is helpful, seeking to lift those who are fallen and to help those who are in need of help. Walking in the Spirit is helpful to other people because we're walking in the light.

If you're walking in the Spirit, some of you are going to have to step up, volunteer, and say, "I'll teach a class. I'll help to lead in this group. I'll assume a place of responsibility. I'll stop being a sponge, soaking up everything that's offered and never giving anything." Walking in the Spirit is a helpful walk, not trying to help yourself, but trying rather to help others. If you're only interested in yourself, you're not walking in the Spirit, you're walking after the flesh. Not because I say so, but because that's what the Book says. This is a helpful walk.

We're to put away the works of darkness. That means that we cannot condone, share, or compromise in evil. We must be light and we must be salt to those who are in sin, always ready to be helpful and never to be harmful.

This walk in the Spirit is helpful because it's marked by boldness. The Spirit has never deserted a believer in a moment of battle with the devil. You're never left alone when you're fighting on God's side. No Christian need be tongue-tied in the presence of sin and evil. The reason for your cowardice and fear is your failure to walk around in the Spirit.

Jesus never promised us freedom from persecution. He promised us boldness. When we are filled with the Spirit, we'll be bold.

One of the most admirable of the Old Testament prophets, in my judgment, is Jeremiah. Brother, he never asked for a time out with sin. He asked for no quarter and gave none. Anywhere sin was found, Jeremiah was there pointing an accusing finger, condemning it, denouncing it. But how do we know Jeremiah today?

We know him as the "weeping prophet." He was bold, he never asked for a time out with sin, but sin broke his heart.

Though we are bold in the faith, our boldness must be tempered with tenderness for we must empathize with those in sin and try to "weep over the erring ones and lift up the fallen."

Thirteen men, chosen by Jesus of Nazareth, changed the course of world history. Those men, thirteen of them with no financial backing, no elaborate organization, no recognition in society, no worldly prestige, no churches in which to meet, no committees from which to receive assistance, transformed the world. They were outnumbered, beaten, persecuted, forbidden to preach, and ultimately put to death. The only answer to their success is that they walked around in the power of God's Holy Spirit.

That's the partnership he offers those who come to him through faith. If you come to Jesus, repenting of your sins, reaching out those feeble hands of faith to receive God's good gift, he'll grant it and he'll give you power to be bold and to succeed for him. That's his offer and the invitation today.

12. Spiritual Perils
1 CORINTHIANS 10:12

Actually, the truths I wish to present are embodied in the text: "Wherefore let him that thinketh he standeth take heed lest he fall." That's the whole thing in a nutshell. The Spirit-filled life is perilous. If you've never understood that, I hope you'll come to grips with this fact. Failure to deal with these perils can result in our repelling, not attracting other people to Jesus Christ. When we fall prey to these spiritual perils, it makes people despise us and laugh at that for which we supposedly stand.

I expect Dr. Peale was correct when he said, "Most of us had rather be ruined by praise than saved by criticism." Criticism is hard to take, isn't it? No matter who gives it, 99 percent of the time we resent it. Criticism can be our most helpful ally when it's given in a spirit of love and helpfulness. Even when it is offered in such a spirit we tend to resist it.

Emily Post once commented that an overdose of praise is like ten lumps of sugar in a cup of coffee, only a few people can swallow it. No matter how it might come, we prefer praise to criticism.

Praise is essential to human personality, but it can be a peril. Children who are overly praised when they are growing up may be as emotionally crippled as those who receive no praise. These are two extremes, then, and those are pitfalls we should avoid.

If there was ever a congregation of Christians on the face of the earth deserving of praise, that congregation is the body of Christ composing First Baptist Church, Wichita Falls, in my judgment. They know I love them and are aware of the fact that I praise them periodically. Yet we can become so addicted to praise that we become like a person on dope. When we need a fix and can't get it, we're beside ourselves. We're helpless. I hope our desire for praise never reaches that point and I hope that my bestowal of praise will always be exactly right; never too much and never too little. To praise too much smacks of insincerity. To praise too little speaks of ingratitude. So with these things in mind and with a sincere desire to avoid pitfalls in both directions let's look at the—

Problem

—that faces us.

The problem is that in living the Spirit-filled life and receiving the richest blessings of heaven individually and collectively, we may come to the point that we think we are deserving, that God has simply given us no more than we ought to have received. I must remind my own heart, as I remind yours, that God has no finished products. No human being on the face of the earth can claim to be exhibit "A" in the process of sanctification saying, "I have arrived." No human reaches the ultimate in Christlikeness in this life.

God has no churches that have arrived. Neither ours nor any other on the face of the earth. Precisely the problem with the seven churches in the Revelation was that they failed to face their true condition. They felt they had arrived. When they did, they sat back at ease in Zion.

Remember the church in Laodicea. Like our own, it was a church composed of wealthy people and it was a wealthy church. I don't care who you are or what your income is, by first-century standards in the church of Laodicea you are far more wealthy than the wealthiest of them. In their wealth they felt that they had need of nothing.

Jesus Christ, the living Son of God, spoke directly to the heart of that church through the apostle John and called them wretched, miserable, poor, blind, and naked. The people in the church of

Laodicea made an entirely different assessment of themselves.

The church in Philadelphia, according to the risen Christ, stood before an open door. Is there any greater heartbreak than that? When God provides a magnificent opportunity for a church and throws open wide the door of challenge for a church, what heartbreak to do as did the one in Philadelphia and stand before the open door. Wouldn't our hearts have been thrilled in the text had said, "The Philadelphians ran through that open door, holding high the banner of the cross and exalting the name of Jesus." But no, they stood before an open door.

Maybe there were members of that congregation who said, "This is just not the time for advance. This is not the moment for a new program. We're not ready for this. This will cause too much chaos for all of us. Let's not move too rapidly." While they were debating the wisdom of passing through the open door, the Spirit of God moved on and they lost their chance.

The church in Sardis had a name to live but they were dead. What a tragedy that is, for a church to be known far and wide as a Bible-believing, Christ-honoring, gospel-preaching church, and then sit back and rest on her laurels and do nothing. They thought everything was alright, but read the condemnation of the living, omniscient Son of God against these churches. A church never reaches a resting place, though a church, a given congregation, may obviously be the recipients of the power of God's Holy Ghost. There's never a moment when we make a truce with Satan. In the moment we try to rest, in the time that we cease our advancement, in that moment the devil wins a major victory.

Strangely enough, even great crowds of worshipers may be a spiritual peril. It is important for a Christian to go to church. It is a Christian's duty to go to church, but it may be a perilous exercise. Now be honest. Have you ever been to church in body only? This occurs when you are physically present, when you sing the songs, read the responsive reading, bow your head as prayers are offered, listen to the sermon, give your offering, and go your way unmoved without any sense of awe or reverence for the presence of the living God in your heart. That's where the peril is found. If you worship and it's only a ritual through which you go, you have missed it all.

Lenin, the Communist leader, has received credit far and wide for the phrase, "Religion is the opiate of the people." Lenin did not originate that phrase. It rather began with a British minister named Charles Kingsley. Kingsley looked about over the community where he preached and all of Britain and discerned the crying need for social reform in England. He saw the church doing absolutely nothing about it. It was Charles Kingsley who cried, "Religion is the opiate of the people." He was saying that for people like you and me to come to church, to attend with regularity, and go our way in a blasé, heedless fashion totally uninvolved in meeting human needs is to be doped by our religious practices. The peril of the church day by day is the possibility of a ritual without life, or worship without a knowledge of the presence of the living God. When that occurs we have succumbed to a grave spiritual peril.

We can give the appearance of devotion to Christ. We can even fool the members of our family. We can fool the ushers at the church. We can fool the deacons. We can fool anybody and everybody humanly speaking, but the Bible says, "God looketh on the heart." Man looks on the outward appearance, but God knows what's down deep on the inside. In the moment that you feel the least need for God's grace and power, in that moment you have succumbed to spiritual peril.

This is an inkling of the problem. Let's look now at spiritual peril represented by our—

Prejudice.

Jesus told us the parable of the lost coin. Remember where it was lost? In the house! What a tragic application can be made of that. In the church house there are people like the lost coin whom the Spirit of God is seeking, seeking, seeking. They haven't gone outside to be lost, but they are inside the house.

In the parable of the older brother, keep in mind that he was lost though he never left home. He stayed at home, but he was lost and never entered into the filial relationship with the father. He never received the joy of salvation and never took the Father's offer of love and sonship.

In another parable Jesus told of two men who went into a temple to pray. You recall the story. One was a Pharisee, the other was a poor, miserable sinner. The one who thought that he was the most spiritual was actually the least. He judged his own spiritual condition by the rituals he had followed. "I fast; I give tithes of all that I possess; I go to church; I'm a good man." The fact that none of these was meaningful is proven in the fact of his attitude toward another worshiper. All of his praying, all of his fasting, all of his tithing, all of his human goodness equals zero because his heart had never been changed! He was still prejudiced against other human beings.

I don't care how long you've worked, how many times you've taught a Sunday School class, how many churches you've served in the capacity of deacon, I don't care how long you've been a member in good standing of a Baptist church. All of that equals zero unless there is a change in your attitude that speaks of the presence of God's Holy Spirit transforming you from the inside. Prejudice is a spiritual peril with which we live every day.

This Pharisee in the parable looked at this other man and said with a smug smile, "I thank thee God that I'm not like other men." He didn't really thank God. There was no thanksgiving in the heart of that man. Prejudice toward other human beings is a cancerous sore that threatens the ministry of any church anywhere. Our church and its membership is open to all people and our congregation includes people of all races. That's good, yet there is prejudice found in the hearts of some of us against certain others.

The designation we sometimes use in an offhand way referring to youngsters as "bus kids" often reveals a hellish, un-Christlike prejudice. In the truest sense, there is absolutely no distinction between "bus kids" and "our kids," and the designation which we ought to use is "God's kids." I don't care what color their skin is. I don't care what part of town they come from. I don't care who their mommas and daddies are, we can't make these neat little divisions between "bus kids" and "our kids." They're God's kids! When the Spirit of the living God dwells in our hearts, we'll be color-blind and will see no difference. God loves those kids "out there" not one whit less than he loves these "in here."

I had a delightful evening recently with my good friend Jerry Clower, from Amite County, Mississippi. Many of you have heard Jerry's recent recordings. I've known him twenty years or more, and we were talking about the problem of prejudice with which we were so familiar in the state of Mississippi. Jerry said with a smile that he had a foolproof method of stopping prejudice. I said, "Man, tell me what it is." He replied, "If God had a little bit of Jerry Clower in him, which he doesn't, he would use my method and stop prejudice overnight." I asked, "What is it?" He answered, "All God would have to do is to turn prejudiced whites black, and turn prejudiced blacks white, and they'd quickly lose their prejudice."

What if you were a black, you who are prejudiced against them, and you were to stand outside wondering whether or not you'd be welcome on the inside? What if you had been pushed to the back of the bus all your life? What if you had been called demeaning names? What if you'd been referred to as something less than human? When we put ourselves in the position of the other man, when we walk a mile in the other man's shoes or even try to, it gives us a new and deeper appreciation for the situation that he faces.

If you're going to be prejudiced against somebody, be prejudiced against something someone can do something about. Be prejudiced against a person who slurps his food when he ought not to. That's something he can change. He can stop that. Be prejudiced, if you will, against your husband for drinking water out of that green bottle instead of pouring it out in a glass. That's something he can stop if properly motivated. Now, that's as much as I'm going to say on that subject! Be prejudiced against something someone can do something about, but don't be prejudiced against a man for the color of his skin. He can't change it! But for the grace of God you would have been born black, or red, or yellow, or some other color than the present color of your skin. Don't despise a person for something he is absolutely powerless to change.

If you want to have prejudice, have prejudice against a person who could do better in business but doesn't because of laziness, lack of desire, lack of ambition, lack of initiative. He can do something about that, but even that kind of prejudice would be short-lived for in a short time we'd go to such a one in love and encourage him to do more and better.

A people as Spirit-filled and heaven-blessed as we must not stumble on the peril of prejudice. Not now nor tomorrow nor in any of the tomorrows that God has given us. We must try, even with major surgery, with a scalpel in the loving hands of the Holy Spirit, to cut out whatever there may be of the cancer of prejudice within our hearts.

Somebody said to me not long ago, "Well, preacher, aren't you prejudiced against those people about whom you're preaching?" I preached a message about some folks who, in my judgment, pervert the doctrine of the Holy Spirit. I said, "No, I'm not prejudiced against those people, but I take my stand against what I construe to be biblical error anywhere, anytime." I don't hate the persons involved, but I hate error and I hate what I judge to be a misinterpretation of the clear teachings of the Word of God. The apostle Paul admonished us to contend earnestly for the faith. We can hate sin, as God does, without hating the sinner, for God hates sin and loves the sinner. That means you and me! Thank God he's not prejudiced. Thank God he doesn't make distinctions such as we make which separate and divide human beings.

The other present peril, as you might have imagined, is—

Pride.

Was it Bob Harrington who said both sin and pride have as their middle letter "I"?

Gnosticism threatened the ministry of the early church. The Gnostics were proud people. They were intellectually *avant-garde*. They claimed that they knew something no one else knew and that they had access to knowledge others were not qualified to receive. That's the kind of pride which can be perilous to God's people.

Some who claim to be Spirit-filled reveal pride in their attempt to impress people with their spirituality. They try to "snow" folks with the fact that they have something special that not everyone has. No one is more repulsive than the individual trying to impress others with his spirituality.

Charles Haddon Spurgeon once said of a young preacher, "I always thought he was humble until he said he was."

After Moses spent forty days with the Lord, the Bible tells us that his countenance shown with a brilliant radiance. But remember the Bible also says about Moses, "He wist not that the skin of his face shown." Moses had been in person-to-person contact with God, alone with God for forty days and forty nights, receiving the diagram for the future of Israel. When Moses came back to the people, he was not aware of the fact that his countenance glowed with heavenly radiance.

Genuine spiritual excellence is totally unselfconscious. By that I'm saying that those that have it don't have to flaunt it. Those that haven't got it have to pretend they have.

This sort of pride is found in the lives of some people who become unteachable. A growing Christian can and should learn from anyone. No Spirit-filled Christian would ever say of another person, "He can't teach me anything." The person who makes that kind of statement has never been more completely enveloped in the hands of Satan.

One preacher in the state of Texas, who has a rather extensive tape ministry, assumes the stance of infallibility, and dismisses anyone who disagrees with him as being uninformed. What a tragedy for a person with so rich a potential to assume the stance of infallibility and say, "I'm right and all others are wrong."

Many, many of God's soldiers have lost their power with God and their influence with man as a result of spiritual pride. It can happen to you, to me, or to any other Christian on the face of the earth. When we reach the point that we think no one else can teach us something, then we've never been more completely in the power of Satan.

James reminded us, "God resisteth the proud but giveth grace to the humble." The Spirit-filled Christian is never presumptuous. He would never hold that the Bible has been opened to him alone and that others don't possess the light that he has. The more we learn, the more hungry-hearted we become and the less and less we feel that we have arrived. The more we can see the heights of our ignorance as we climb the mountain of understanding. No one has ever walked so close to the Lord for so long a time that he's no longer subject to being deceived.

No one of us will ever come to a plateau in life where we need not fear the devil. To think we've reached such a plateau is to be in deep spiritual peril. When a Christian becomes self-confident and cocky, he's in prime position for real defeat.

Ours is a spectator world. Throngs go out to football games, but they don't play. Multitudes go to the theater, but they do not sing or act. Huge crowds come to church, but they never become participants in the work of the Kingdom. Don't allow your spiritual pride to keep you from getting up to your elbows in the hard, menial tasks involved in proclaiming the gospel, in exalting Jesus Christ, and growing in knowledge of him.

We have on our church roll hundreds of members, able bodied and in good health, who are not enrolled in Bible study. They may be totally ignorant in the Word of God. They may not even know the first or the last book of the Bible, but they are saying by their unwillingness to participate in Bible study, "I already know all I want to know." What an awesome tragedy, for what a dangerous position that is to hold.

There are some of you who have adequate Bible knowledge to share with others who desperately need to step to the front, volunteer, and take your place in a teaching, learning ministry. There will never be a more opportune moment than right now.